James Oswald Dykes

The Relations of the Kingdom to the World

James Oswald Dykes

The Relations of the Kingdom to the World

ISBN/EAN: 9783337183653

Printed in Europe, USA, Canada, Australia, Japan

Cover: Foto ©Lupo / pixelio.de

More available books at **www.hansebooks.com**

THE

RELATIONS OF THE KINGDOM TO THE WORLD.

BY

J. OSWALD DYKES, D.D.

Οὐκ ἐρωτῶ ἵνα ἄρῃς αὐτοὺς ἐκ τοῦ κόσμου, ἀλλ' ἵνα τηρήσῃς αὐτοὺς ἐκ τοῦ πονηροῦ.—JOHN XVII. 15.

NEW YORK:
ROBERT CARTER & BROTHERS.
1874.

PREFATORY NOTE.

Deeply conscious of the imperfect success which has attended his attempt to open up that great Sermon which is the Lord's own MANIFESTO OF THE KINGDOM OF GOD, *the Author ventures, nevertheless, to offer this concluding portion to such readers as may have found any profit from the two preceding parts, on* 'THE BEATITUDES,' *and on* 'THE LAWS OF THE KINGDOM.'

INTRODUCTION.

A

INTRODUCTION.

THE main or central mass of our Lord's teaching in this Sermon has been already considered by us.[1] It consists in a republication of Mosaic law under its 'fulfilled' form; that is, with its literal precepts translated into spiritual principles of virtue, resumed under one comprehensive canon of godlike love, and animated by the supreme religious motive of regard for the approval of our heavenly Father. In laying down for His new kingdom such a 'fulfilled' edition of Hebrew morals, Jesus could not escape a running polemic against those accepted teachers of His time who had done their best, not to fulfil, but to destroy, the ancient law of which they boasted to be the guardians, and were the recognised expositors. But the spiritual kingdom, whose foundations our Lord was here laying, though it grew out of the bosom of the Mosaic system, and, above all, drew from that system what had been its main glory— its ethical law—was yet destined to attain an in-

INTRO-
DUCTION.

Matt. v. 17–
vi. 18.

---

[1] In a volume entitled, *The Laws of the Kingdom*. Nisbet & Co. 2d ed. 1873.

dependent position, and to hold relations with a wider world than the little realm of Israel. The last great section of the Sermon, therefore, on which we are now entering, contains a series of rules for christian life, which (though admitted to be less vigorously knit into a unity than what precedes) may be described as all bearing on the relations of the kingdom of God to the existing condition, not of Judaism only, but of every society on earth,—to the 'world,' as it is to be found at all times and in every land. From this point, therefore, the discourse shows less of its local and Hebrew colouring. It wears less the aspect of a rejoinder to the Rabbinical schools. It deals, not with Mosaic law or ritual, but with the great facts of catholic human life. How the christian disciple stands to this world as an object of desire or of possession; what attitude he is to assume towards its sin, whether within or without the christian brotherhood; by what means men may pass from the evil world outside into the little kingdom of the saved; and how evil, which has stolen under disguise into the very kingdom of God, is to be detected:—such are the points with which this closing section is occupied. They all cluster round one central theme—the relations of the Kingdom to the world.

Wherever men of very strong religious nature have set themselves vigorously to the task of gathering around them a select community of disciples, who shall lead a purer and more pious life than is led by the bulk of mankind, there has been developed a strong tendency towards a literal and social segregation from common life. To separate from the sins of life without actually abandoning to some extent its ties and duties, has never appeared possible, or at least sufficient; and the crown of merit has therefore been in nearly every great religion reserved for those few ardent devotees whose zeal enables them to break with society. Vows of poverty or celibacy, retreats, religious communities, and brotherhoods of every description, are only so many ways of accomplishing that outward severance from the world, without which a spiritual deliverance from its temptations and impurities is despaired of; and these have been the resource of the mistaken pious under every faith. In Buddhist monasteries, in the Fakirs of Brahminism and the Hadjis of the Moslem faith, not less than in Hebrew Essenes, Catholic convents, and Moravian settlements, we trace the widespread fruits of one profound conviction of deep thinkers on religion, that to attain to the kingdom of God a man must needs go out of the world. It is one of the most striking peculiarities of the religion which rests on Holy Scripture, that, almost alone among the great faiths of history, it repudiates this maxim. Neither in its Hebrew nor in its Christian sacred books, do we find social separation proposed as an aid to piety. Moses framed his institutes for a commonwealth in which patriotism and religion became almost identified. Christ designed His Church to be a society standing aloof only in a spiritual sense from the world, while penetrating and inhabiting it. As little countenance as Essenism found in the Pentateuch, so little does cœnobitic or celibate life, whether under Catholic or Protestant names, find in the Gospels. The kingdom of heaven, of which this Sermon is the earliest manifesto, was not to be *of* this world in its moral or spiritual temper; but it certainly was to be, in the fullest possible sense, *in* this world; 'fulfilling' (here again), and not 'destroying,' those domestic, civil, and social moulds into which the original design of God meant human life to run.

To such a society, its right relations to ordinary secular life become, it is obvious, of exceptional importance. Those relations must be mainly of two sorts. In the first instance, the world is a

marginalia:
INTRODUCTION.

Cf. 1 Cor. v. 9, 10, vii. 20, 31.

John xvii. 15–18.

Introduction.

place to live in; and the christian disciple, who is not to abandon the possession of property, but continues bound to provide the means of subsistence for himself and his family, finds himself at once face to face with a crowd of questions turning on the right or wrong acquisition, preservation, and employment of wealth. This is the large subject handled by our Lord in the first paragraph of this section. In the next place, the world is a seat and source of moral evil. The heavenly kingdom, if it exist in the presence of evil, must exist as a witness against it, striving to shame the evil, and win men from it; and to do this wisely asks special prudence. Notwithstanding its witness, the world will always number the vast majority of mankind; and the effort of the few to attain for themselves super-worldly purity or nobleness must be proportionately severe. Besides, evil men and their evil influences cannot be wholly kept out of a society which is not to be locally separate; and the danger of gradual deterioration or wholesale swamping of the little kingdom of good by such incursions from the great world of evil outside, is a danger which must be faced. On all these questions our Lord gives enduring instructions in the latter portion of this section. The links between its several minor

INTRO-
DUCTION.

Matt. vi. 19-34.

vii. 1-6.

vii. 7-14.

vii. 15-23.

INTRO-
DUCTION.

paragraphs do not always lie on the surface; but the general drift of this third main division of the Sermon on the Mount seems to be hardly less obvious than that of the two earlier, which have already been considered in previous volumes.

PART I.
RELATIONS TO THE WORLD AS A POSSESSION.

AGAINST COVETOUSNESS.

Lay not up for yourselves treasures upon earth, where moth and rust doth corrupt, and where thieves break through and steal; but lay up for yourselves treasures in heaven, where neither moth nor rust doth corrupt, and where thieves do not break through nor steal: for where your treasure is, there will your heart be also. The light of the body is the eye: if therefore thine eye be single, thy whole body shall be full of light. But if thine eye be evil, thy whole body shall be full of darkness. If therefore the light that is in thee be darkness, how great is that darkness! No man can serve two masters: for either he will hate the one, and love the other; or else he will hold to the one, and despise the other. Ye cannot serve God and mammon.— MATT. VI. 19–24 ; cf. LUKE XII. 33, 34, XI. 34–36, XVI. 13.

AGAINST COVETOUSNESS.

H OW a subject of the kingdom of heaven ought to hold himself related to worldly property, is the point determined for us by the King, in the paragraph which fills the remainder of this sixth chapter. Questions of detail are not discussed; but the axe is laid to the root of two errors, lying on either hand of the christian disciple. As, in the later-spoken parable of the Sower, those thorns which choke the seed in even the best soil are described as of two species—the one 'the care of this world,' and the other 'the deceitfulness of riches;' so here, the lot of rich and poor is viewed as equally beset, though by an opposite peril. On one side lies avarice, the idolatrous delight of the possessor in his possessions, and his strange craving to add to them. On the other, lies over-anxious fear for want, and the distrustful care about to-morrow. Opposed as they are, however, and besetting opposite social classes, these two faults meet in this, that both alike obscure the spiritual sense for divine truth, and steal the dominion of the soul from God. Both covetous-

PART I.

FIRST WARNING.

Cf. Matt. xii 22 and parallels.

Vers. 22-24.

-ness and anxiety make the inner eye evil, and set up a rival master over the will. Alike, therefore, and equally, they contradict the Christian's fundamental relationship to his Father in heaven. Alike, and equally, they traverse the supreme example of our King, Who, when He was rich enough to be God's equal, was so far from grasping at that as His 'treasure,' that, for our sakes, He humbled Himself and became poor; yet, in His day of poverty, had so little unworthy dread of want, that He still knew how 'the Father had given all things into His hands,' and was able to say: 'All Thine are Mine.' Neither of those social extremes, from which a wise old Hebrew prayed to be kept, will succeed in corrupting the simplicity of that man's piety, who not only hears the words, but also has imbibed the spirit, of Jesus Christ.

[margin: PART I. FIRST WARNING.]
[margin: 2 Cor. viii. 9; c. Phil. ii. 6, 7, Greek.]
[margin: John iii. 35, xiii. 3, xvii. 10.]
[margin: Prov. xxx. 8, 9.]

Our Lord's first warning is against the overprizing of earthly possessions. It is expressed with intentional largeness of language. 'Treasure not treasures for yourselves' is a phrase which need by no means be narrowed to money. It covers whatever men value most highly, and, because they value it most highly, take most pains to increase, if it be capable of increase, or to pre-

[margin: Matt. vi. 19, Greek.]

serve, if it stand in risk of loss. Nor need there be any reference intended to the intrinsic value of the thing; for our human hearts have the most pathetic habit of clothing worthless objects with an ideal preciousness, and throwing away their love and care on that which is contemptible. A 'treasure' is simply each man's *summum bonum;* his darling; that to which, be it noble or vile, he has elected to cling as his best thing, over which he hangs with doating pride, from which he tries to suck his chief delight, and for which, if you offer to rob him of it, he will do most desperate battle. Our Lord gives us the best insight into the wide meaning of His words, when He defines a 'treasure' as something which draws the heart after it. These words of the twenty-first verse, 'Where your treasure is, there will your heart be also,' carry indeed some deeper lesson for us; but on the face of them, they do at least tell us what a 'treasure' is; and that no acquiring of possessions, nor amassing of them, will turn them into treasures, unless we consent to give them a too forward and large room within our affections. If we do, there is nothing so lofty or worthy of our love but Christ's words will smite it; just as there is nothing so sordid or paltry but men's love may over-prize it.

PART I.

FIRST WARNING.

Ver. 21.

PART I.
FIRST
WARNING.

Cf. Ezra ii. 69;
Neh. vii. 70;
Job xxvii. 16;
Isa. l. 9; Jas.
v. 2, 3.

There is, however, one species of possession on which people have agreed to bestow the exclusive name of 'riches;' and our Lord's words about the rust and moth show of what sort of treasures He was most directly thinking. Such treasures as the moth can eat—those rich suits of superfluous apparel with which the opulent Oriental has always been accustomed to fill his wardrobe; such treasures as rust can fret—all rare or costly ornaments, like metals of price and splendour; treasures which thieves can dig for to steal, like jars of hoarded coin buried in the earth or concealed within the household safe: these, in a land where banks are unknown, and landed property not always to be had, are the natural equivalents for our modern forms of wealth. It indicates how prevailingly the heart of man is set on property, whether in kind or currency, that this wide word 'treasure' has come to be almost exclusively appropriated by that one class of precious things which are material and of the earth; just as we call our perishable and marketable merchandise by the name of 'goods,' as if nothing else were so good as they. To most men, nothing so readily becomes a treasure as money. Nothing wields so wide a fascination, or subjects so many human souls to an abject servitude, as money. In no age has the pursuit of money been made the end of life by a larger number of civilised men, or professed by them to be the end of their life with more frank audacity, than in this age. The words of Jesus are therefore so far from obsolete, that, spoken though they were long ago, and by an Oriental to Orientals, no words could possibly be more in place when addressed to the christian business men of England at this very moment than these words: Lay not up for yourselves such treasures as these; of all objects of human desire or delight, make not wealth your treasure; 'take heed and beware of covetousness.'

PART I.
FIRST WARNING.

Luke xii. 15.

Christ's popular didactic style rejected all saving clauses; yet it need hardly be said, that though His words stand unrestricted, 'Treasure no treasures,' He cannot mean to forbid or blame every kind of hoarding and saving; such, for example, as that 'laying up' by parents for their children which St. Paul commends as a duty. 2 Cor. xii. 14. Reasonable thrift, or a certain measure of economy in living, which, without degenerating into parsimony, makes prudent provision against the future, is not permissible only, but dutiful. The improvement of one's means with a view to secure more than competence, even opulence, in the

PART I.
FIRST
WARNING.

hope of thereby attaining a wider power to serve God and benefit society; this also is, to say the least, permissible. For some men it may even be a laudable ambition. What is in every case forbidden, is such amassing of money, or endeavours to amass it, as must engross affections which ought to be fixed on nobler and diviner objects; such amassing as makes of money the 'treasure' of the heart.

Perhaps few persons, who have not looked with some keenness into character, have any suspicion how strong and general is the fascination which is exercised over average natures by the sense of property. To call anything for the first time one's own, is to awaken to a new power, and experience a vivid delight; as you may see by the clutch of almost infant fingers on the coin you give them. To feel that what one has can grow; that money well used will breed money; that in the process of gaining, there is opened a path of delightful activity practically endless: this is for many young men in our day the first seductive and perilous discovery of their lives. The stimulant of money-making, with its exciting hazards and the zest which competition lends to it, may become first delicious, then intoxicating, and at length indispensable, just like any other stimulant. The growth of this appetite is no less easy or insidious, and it is far more unobserved and unrebuked by public opinion, than the appetite for drink or gaming. Our own generation has witnessed the spectacle of whole communities driven to frenzy for a time by a gold fever. There is no generation but has seen individual cases of moral insanity induced from the same cause. Those cases in which the love of money for its own sake has come to eat up all other loves which at the first were mingled with it, such as love of speculation, love of display, love of the deference men pay the rich, or love of the luxuries money can procure; till the poor hoarder hardens and shrivels into that meanest of human creatures, whose wretchedness and despicableness are both stamped upon the very name of 'miser' which we give him;—such cases, I say, are, happily for human nature, always rare. But the sin of avarice—the sin of erecting property into a 'treasure' of the heart—assumes countless shapes less repulsive than that. In truth, it seldom appears alone, and never appears so all at once. Characters of men are not such simple things that you can describe them in a word. This particular vice enters readily into combination with vanity, with ambition, with luxury, with mere delight in successful

PART I.
FIRST WARNING.

activity. It hides itself, too, under the specious cloak of diligence in business, or of foresight, or of a desire to be generous and bountiful; and in such disguise, it may too easily escape detection by the man himself, whose soul it is darkening and enslaving. Yet even as thus modified or disguised, it is in its essence what St. Paul twice calls it, an 'idolatry,' and in its issue a fertile 'root of all evils.' He who, in an age like the present—almost in any age—would keep his soul from this poison, and yet conduct with diligence and success the business of life, has need both to watch narrowly the state of his own heart, and to study the workings of the evil in the men around him. To speak the truth, money, in every one of its bearings, is a thing of peril. To desire to gain it, especially to gain it fast, is perilous: because the rising man of business, who has his fortune to make, and is in haste to make it, is on a road strewn thick with lies and roguery, with tricks, conspiracies, and speculations which exceed the bounds of prudence; and it is hard indeed to devote the energies of body and soul, by day and night, to one end with such intensity as the making of a fortune does now ordinarily demand, without coming to attach an altogether unreasonable value to the gains which have cost so much.

How easily does a hard-won fortune become the 'treasure' of the winner's life! To have made money is nearly as perilous as to desire it. The merchant who has spent life in acquiring, ends it commonly in spending; but having forgotten to learn how to spend it well, he runs the risk of either falling into self-indulgent luxury, like that of Dives in the parable, or of wasting his substance in vulgar display. Designing to purchase for himself the reputation of a man of means and elegance, he may in reality earn only the character of a purse-proud upstart. Nor is it much less perilous to inherit than to gain a fortune. The complacency of the proprietor who reposes on the winnings of a dead ancestor, his pride of family, his envy of older or richer houses, and his chuckle of quiet contempt for the 'self-made' man, betray an idolatry to his patrimonial treasures as deep as any. Take it how you will, in fact, with what varieties of surrounding your knowledge of the world may suggest to you, wealth is everywhere the most insidious and fascinating and dangerous of all those things which steal away the souls of men to become their 'treasure' and their idol. It were better for any man who finds himself entangled in that mesh whose threads are of gold, to alienate his superfluous gains by one supreme

PART I.

FIRST WARNING.

Luke xvi. 19 ff.

PART I.
FIRST WARNING.

Matt. v. 30, and parallels.

Vers. 19, 20.

act of sacrifice, cutting off for the Kingdom of Heaven's sake the 'right hand,' which has learnt to clutch too eagerly or hold too fast the treasures of the earth.

Nor is this idolatry even a very wise or noble one among the idolatries of mankind. Sundry reasons against making money our treasure are enforced by our blessed Lord in this strong dissuasive of His; but the first and simplest is insinuated in the very words of the warning itself. It is a poor sort of treasure which perishes so soon, and perishes so meanly too, as do our earthly gains. Money has no manner of divineness about it, either inherent or representative. The ancient Greek or modern Hindu, who has conceived a divinity of some sort to be imaged for him by the statue in the shrine, does a nobler thing when he bows before that semblance or remembrancer of what is the highest, wisest, and best he knows,—the sum, to his belief, of superhuman and unchanging excellence,—than they do, who, in the commercial idolatry of England, sacrifice their spiritual capacities, and what is divinest in their hearts, to money-making. For what is this same money? Not by any one supposed to be at all divine, or to bear any manner of relation to any Power holier than myself; no emblem to us of Him Who is worthy of worship: but a very poor and swift-perishing bit of earth; one of the meanest of the creatures made to minister to the physical necessities of the least of us. At its best, it is a slave ordained to serve the transient wants of the body, and then, like the body which it serves, to die and pass: no more. The moth which eats into the silken tissues of the East and makes out of their brilliant folds only a fretwork of decay; the thief who digs an entrance to the ill-guarded pot of gold through the Oriental's house of clay, are emblems of that inevitable insecurity which attaches to all earthly property, and of that waste which must one day dissipate its preciousness. What we moderns invest in trade or in the funds, is as liable to 'make itself wings' as the treasures of an eastern home. It was the nature of such material property as men stored up of old, to lose by flux of time; and although in modern mercantile affairs one may object that it is, on the contrary, a quality of wealth to increase itself, still it can only be increased by being risked. The faster you desire to make it grow, the greater likelihood you run of losing it through chance of trade or fraud of men. Make nothing by your capital; it wastes, slowly but surely, by mere expenditure, or at any rate, by depreciation

PART I.

FIRST WARNING.

Prov. xxiii. 5.

PART I. in its relative value: make much by it, and you
FIRST WARNING. chance the loss of all. You can only avoid the
'rust' by exposing it to the 'thief.' Above all,
it is to be remembered that we are more perishable than our goods. If we could remain, they would go. If they remain, at least we go. We
Job xiii. 28. are such creatures as 'consume like a garment that is moth-eaten;' and each of us could name one crowned and sceptred thief, who shall ere
Cf. 2 Cor. v. 1. long dig through the clay walls of our mortal house, to rob us of our treasures in robbing us of our life. When death takes a man's breath away, it takes his purse as well; disinherits him of his lands; unrobes him of earthly raiment; and despatches him, lonely, naked, shivering, a poor despoiled ghost, into the unknown. In that day, when the head which presses a pillow of down and is laved by jewelled fingers, lies no easier in its death-sweat than any other; in that day, when the gathered treasures of a whole lifetime are slipping through the unwilling grasp, to go to other hands that are no less greedy, and a land must be entered where gold and purple are words unheard: then, surely, in the desolation of all earthly delight and the scattering for ever of earth's hoarded gain, shall these words return, like a too-late reproach in dying ears: 'Lay not up for

Against Covetousness.

yourselves treasures upon earth, but lay up for yourselves treasures in heaven, where neither moth nor rust doth corrupt, and where thieves do not break through nor steal.'

There is a better use, our Lord would have us understand, to be made of our wealth, than make a treasure of it. As He taught expressly in the parable of the Unjust Steward, so He probably desired to insinuate here, that money well spent on earth for God and for His kingdom will be found at last to be well-spent money indeed, transmuted in the rewards of heaven into an imperishable treasure. However this may be, He does at least set over against the precious things of this life another description of gains, the enjoyment of which is reserved for a life to come. It is not only by a conscientious and charitable administration of our income, but by every act of affectionate devotion to God and to His will, that we are to lay up for ourselves rewards against the heavenly state. That commendation by the Father in secret which our Lord has just been promising to every genuine worshipper, extends itself to all christian obedience and the whole service of a faithful life. Nor is it to end in barren commendation, but to entail a rich, though as yet un-

PART I.

FIRST WARNING.

Luke xvi. 1-12; cf. Matt. xix. 21 (words which occur in Luke's version of our text: s. xii. 33). Also 1 Tim. vi. 18, 19.

Matt. vi. 1, 4, 6, 18.

PART I.
FIRST
WARNING.

1 Pet. i. 4.

Luke xii. 21.

known 'reward.' The sum of all such rewards of grace, laid up meanwhile in the just purposes of the heavenly Judge, shall be one day the everlasting possession, the incorruptible and unfading inheritance, of the sons of God. This is for man the true riches—riches toward God; and on such treasures Jesus would have His followers set their hearts. So to earn money as in the upright labour by which we earn it to please the Father; so to save money as in the purpose and temper with which we save it to please the Father; so to spend money as in the use to which we put it and the good we do by it, to please the Father; but ever to keep it in its place as our servant and the Father's gift, a trust to be neither rejoiced in for its own sake nor squandered in its superfluity on vain personal delight, but diligently to be put to holy service in the honouring of Him and the comforting of His children: this is the attitude our Master would plainly have us hold to this needful though perilous possession. This is to turn a base thing not only to honest, but even to noble use. This is to exchange earthly wealth for a heavenly treasure.

It is only when a soul has become inflamed with a passion for those divine rewards which are as yet only promised, not tasted, and is upheld by patient faith in such riches to come, that it can afford to spurn for the sake of God the seduction of gold. For men who are already rich, and have learned to pride themselves on their riches, it is so hard to enter the kingdom of God as to be the next thing to impossible. Even men like those whom Christ was addressing on the mount, who were as yet poor, and, while poor, had already entered that kingdom, were still in danger from a new-born lust to gain and to own a portion in this life. While He addressed them, He may have seen in the hearts of these peasants whom He had just made princes in the kingdom of the Messiah, a dawning of covetousness as well as of ambition—a hope stirring blindly within them, that to follow this King might prove to be the path to fortune not less than to honour. At any cost, such a seduction must be in christian hearts withstood. During the course of His earnest dissuasive against laying up treasures on earth, He had insinuated one indirect argument in support of His prohibition, drawn from the perishableness of what is earthly. To any one who has so much as realized his own immortality, it must appear foolish, to say no more, and unworthy of himself, to gather wealth which is corruptible and transitory instead of such as shall

PART I.

FIRST WARNING.

Mark x. 23-27.

last him for ever. But our Lord does not trust to the influence of this single consideration. The passion for gold wins its hold too easily and keeps it too tenaciously, even on christian hearts, to be subdued by an argument drawn from the remote, unworldly future. Therefore our Teacher proceeds to adduce in quick succession no fewer than three additional and more express reasons against the amassing of earthly treasures; reasons, every one of which is drawn from the damage which the treasuring of such treasures must inflict even now upon the spiritual life of a christian disciple. Our Lord is speaking to men who are already in His kingdom; who not only look for the rewards of the Father in some better state after death, but who profess to care, more than for anything else, to have the Father's rule set up within them in this present life, to see God's face here below, to walk within His light, and to fill their hearts with His love. And He warns them, that to prize earthly gains for their own sake, or hunt after them and hoard them, is not only to forfeit the future rewards of heaven, but it is to drag the heart itself down from heaven to earth; it is to cloud or distort the soul's vision of God; it is to dethrone the Father, and become a vassal to a baser lord. That Jesus should have deemed it

Against Covetousness. 29

wise to pursue this golden idol with so many redoubled blows, proves how close and urgent was the danger of such idolatry even in the case of the apostles. The busy money-makers of this generation are at least no less exposed to such a danger than that handful of Galilean operatives can have been, who sat round a Galilean carpenter to hear these words; and therefore it will be well worth our pains to look a little closely at those three evils to spiritual life which are here traced directly to the love, or even to the amassing, of money.

PART I.
FIRST WARNING.

1. I say, 'even to the amassing of money;' for, by His first objection to earthly treasures, I understand our Lord to mean that the very heaping up of worldly wealth draws men to love it. 'Where thy treasure is,' He says, 'there will thy heart be also.'[1] It is true that, in the pregnant ethical sense in which our Lord chiefly intends the word, a thing does not become a man's treasure, no matter how much he may have of it, until it has drawn his heart to itself. At the same time, the word 'treasure' only receives this pregnant ethical signification in the second place.

Ver. 21.

See above, p. 15.

---

[1] The best critical editions read σου; not ὑμῶν, as in Luke xii. 34.

PART I.
FIRST
WARNING.

It primarily means anything laid up or amassed; any superfluous possession, stored for delight or for the future, rather than for immediate use. Now there is an important moral fact shadowed forth by this deepening of the word's signification. What one treasures, in the primary sense, tends to become his treasure in the deeper sense. It draws his heart after it. Every possession which a man likes to have without using it, and lays past for the pride of having it, and strives continually to increase, may be a harmless enough treasure at first, so long as his interest in it remains quite subordinate; but its tendency is more and more to draw him into itself, to engage his interest more deeply, and become more precious in his eyes. Of course, this proneness to doat upon any possession is strengthened by the pains we take to add to it, or the sacrifices we must incur in order to preserve it. The fortune which a busy man toils late and early to augment, and for the sake of which his head has been blanched with anxiety; or the estate which is purchased at the expense of what ought to have been patrimony to his younger children, only that he may feel the pride of proprietorship: these possessions have acquired a fictitious dearness through the heavy price which they have cost. But this is not all. The mere laying up and keeping by us of anything which is superfluous, whether it cost much or not, whether we are adding to its costliness or not, has a certain quality of seductiveness about it, provided only we cherish either joy or pride in the possession of it. There is nothing wrong, then, in the joyful or proud possession of what is rare or lovely or for any reason precious? No, not of necessity, by any means. But there must always be danger at least in the amassing of such property; danger that the joy of possession will come to intoxicate and seduce the heart. Only to have a very great deal of any precious thing; to make a store of it, and be proud of it; still more, to consult much how to secure it, or toil much to add to it; whether the treasure be so noble as influence or knowledge, or so petty as a drawerful of curiosities, or so common as a little wealth: this is to run the risk of having the heart narrowed by degrees, and lowered to that region of life where the treasure lies.

Against such a danger the Christian must be continually on his guard. It is taken for granted, what no Christian will question, that his supreme love, pride, joy, desire—in one word, his 'heart'— is due to Him Who is above, and to those things of His which are above; to God, and the pleasing of

PART I.
FIRST WARNING.

PART I.
FIRST WARNING.
Cf. Col. iii. 2;
Phil. iii. 20.

God, and the fulfilment of the will, and the increase of the honour, of God. What St. Paul in his companion letters to Colosse and Philippi has expressly insisted on, is here by St. Paul's Master still more strikingly assumed. The heart of a disciple of Christ will come to be with his treasures on the earth, if he once suffer himself to lay up for himself any such treasures; and that, you feel that the Master feels, is a self-refuting and preposterous issue to a disciple's earthly treasuring. It belongs to the very idea of a Christian, that what he sets his heart on cannot be here at all,

Cf. Eph. ii. 6.

but must be above in the heavenly places, among the incorruptibles. There is no need in his case for any *Sursum corda!* His heart is on high. But there is need still for the warning: Treasure no treasures below; for earthly treasures drag down heavenly hearts. 'Where thy treasure is, there will thy heart be also.'

The next two reasons for abstaining from storing earth's precious things are expressed under a metaphorical dress; and although in both cases the explanation of the metaphor is appended, yet the abruptness with which these sentences are introduced, and their apparent remoteness at first sight from the train of thought hitherto followed, have occasioned some difficulty in determining the inner connection of the passage. Let it be kept in view, that the Preacher's design is to dissuade His followers from amassing wealth, by tracing its evil effects on the spiritual life. Its first natural effect we have seen to be the down-dragging of the heart from its celestial object to settle around its earthly gains. Now, the central ideas in the next two sentences are, first the darkening, and then the enslavement, of the soul. But it needs no acuteness to perceive that these two are the most obvious of all consequences from such a degradation of the affections as He has just spoken of. Only let the heart be kept down to the earthly sphere through those treasures which a man has laid up for himself, so that his chief interest is no longer in God, but in his gold; and it must follow, (1) that his spiritual vision for divine truth will become obscured, and (2) that gold will take the place of God as the real master of the man's practical life. In other words, the displacement of God from the seat of the affections acts injuriously, both on the faculty of spiritual insight, and on the loyalty of the will to duty.

PART I.

FIRST WARNING.

2. The amassing of money, then, has led to the love of money; and the first thing which the love

Vers. 22, 23.

PART I.
───
FIRST
WARNING.

See John i. 9,
viii. 12, ix. 5,
xii. 35, 36, 46;
and cf. 1 Thess.
v. 5; Eph. v.
14; 2 Cor. iv.
4–6; 1 John i.
5–7, ii. 8–11.

of money does is to put out the eye of the soul. For the spiritual nature, as our Lord everywhere taught, has its own faculty of vision, just as the body has. What the sun does for the enlightenment of our physical life, so that we can recognise the objects by which we are surrounded in this world and order our movements with regard to them, God, revealing Himself to us in His Son Jesus, does for the moral and religious life of men. By the truth which shines in the face of Him Who is 'the Light of the world,' each one who will may always realize divine facts and things, which are none the less real for being immaterial, and may walk no longer, as a spiritual being, in the dark, but in the light. Only the condition of such spiritual illumination, as of physical, is, that the organ by which we see God be kept healthy. Faith is the spiritual equivalent of vision; and

See Matt. v. 8. it is the pure heart alone which so believes as to see God. In other words, this faculty of spiritual insight, or receptivity of the soul for moral and religious truth, depends upon the simplicity or integrity of the man's spiritual nature, that is to say, upon the whole-heartedness with which he loves and desires God. To love God is to be able to see His light; to let one's love fall upon a base earthly treasure, is to hurt the most sensitive and necessary of our spiritual faculties; it is to trouble the eye of the soul, to confuse its vision of divine things as they are, and in the end to destroy the action of that 'faith' which is 'the evidence,' the realizing perception, of things unseen.

Our Lord's parable becomes now, by the help of His use of similar imagery elsewhere, very clear indeed. 'The eye,' He says, 'is the lamp of the body;' not the ultimate source of its light, but its centre of enlightenment; a kind of miniature and second-hand luminary, or light-bringer, to all the rest of our physical organs, without which, as in blind people, all the bodily life is darkened, like a house by night without a candle. The condition of enlightenment is the soundness of this little tender organ : if it be 'right,' or in a normal state, the whole body is, as it were, lit up; whereas if it be 'bad,' in a diseased condition, it matters not what sunshine may flood the earth, your body will be all darkened, like a house without a window. Now, then, comes the application of the parable. 'In thee,' says Jesus to His christian disciple, there is also 'light,' through the organ of spiritual vision, whose power depends upon its moral soundness, singleness, and simplicity. By it, when in spiritual health, thou canst see God, and in His light canst see all things clearly.

PART I.
FIRST WARNING.

Heb. xi. 1, Greek.

ὁ λύχνος, ver 22.

ἁπλοῦς.

πονηρός.

τὸ φῶς.

Cf. Ps xxxvi 9.

PART I.
FIRST WARNING.

τὸ ϲκότος.

Then the naturally dark appetencies and passions of thy lower nature are illuminated, and guided to their proper service, along their bounded paths; and all the inner life is made orderly, conscious, bright, and healthful. But if even this divine light that is in thee be turned again to darkness, through the disordering of that spiritual organ, how great, alas! shall be the darkness of 'the dark' itself; of that lower animal nature, whose blind appetites are no longer ruled by the insight which was wont to guide, or checked by the illumination which was wont to shame them!

Our Lord has not said here, that it is the degradation of a Christian's affection to earthly property which, by destroying the singleness, impairs the sensitiveness of his spiritual vision; and perhaps He has only not said so, because it does not really matter what idol divides our affections with the things above. No divided or impure heart whatever can clearly and steadily see the light of God. But we do not need to be told what a darkening influence is exercised over christian men by the love of money in particular. We are unhappily too familiar with its ravages in the modern church: with disciples, genuine enough, zealous sometimes to a fault, and loud in their profession of Christianity, who nevertheless betray, by the stationariness of their moral character, or by their unconscious perseverance in faulty habits which every one notices but themselves, or by overlooking very obvious duties lying in their path, that they cannot be walking open-eyed in the light of God. Christians who throughout the greater part of life remain unchastened, ungentle, unmellowed, hardly distinguishable from the utter worldling by reason of their petty, grasping, saving ways, are frequent enough everywhere. Were the cause of such blear-eyed religion to be faithfully inquired after, or could it be plainly told, how often would it prove to be just this— that the real desire of their heart is not bent with single-minded longing upon the attainment of God's approval or of His celestial rewards, but has become diverted to an excessive degree on temporal objects, chained down to earth and made earthy by the over-eager pursuit of success, or by an over-warm delight in such perishable gains as they have been able to win for themselves in the scramble of business! With such Christians a reverse process has been going on from that which happened to the converts of Ephesus. The eyes of those hearts at Ephesus were enlightened, so that they saw the riches of God's own inheritance —the celestial wealth destined for children of

Eph. i. 18, Greek, corrected text.

God in the everlasting kingdom of their Father. But we suffer the dazzle of corruptible gold to fall across our vision, and draw after it the worship of the heart; then our eyes which were full of heaven's own light grow dim again, the celestial glory fades away, the shining crown suspended over christian heads has leave to hang there unseen, and we toil on to rake together in the dark what is but dust after all, though it be the dust of gold.[1]

Ver. 24.

3. There is a more disastrous fate still in store for the disciple who falls under the fascination of gain. Loss of sight, or a gradual obscuring of that eye of the heart which looks upward and sees God, is accompanied, on the practical side of life, by captivity of the will. The image here used by our Lord is transparent enough; and yet the force of His language has been a good deal lost in translation, through that happy change which since He spoke has lightened the condi-

---

[1] 'The Interpreter takes them apart again, and has them first into a room where was a man that could look no way but downwards, with a muck-rake in his hand: there stood also One over his head with a celestial crown in His hand, and proffered him that crown for his muck-rake; but the man did neither look up nor regard, but did rake to himself the straws, the small sticks, and the dust of the floor.'—*Pilgrim's Progress*, Part II.

tions of servitude, and made all words to describe the obedience of man to man less grievous to the ear. We are so far removed from every association with slavery, that when we read, 'No man can serve two masters,' we think only of such voluntary service as one free-born Englishman may contract to pay another. The language carries a vastly harsher sense. The service of which Jesus spoke, and which His hearers understood Him to mean, was the utter subjection of a bond-slave to the mere will—the almost unchecked caprice—of a slave-lord. This impossibility which He so sharply emphasizes, is that which any domestic[1] slave would encounter who should endeavour to hold himself at the beck of two different lords, each at the head of a separate and independent household. That the two lords are assumed to have contrasted jurisdictions, and to issue contrary orders, is obvious. In fact, if the orders of both coincided, there would in reality be only one lordship, one rule. Let it be noticed, however, that this alleged impossibility of executing the will of two contrary masters is not made to depend on the physical obstacle, that a slave cannot be in two households or do two diverse

---

[1] Cf. οἰκέτης in the parallel passage in Luke (xvi. 13) under a different connection.

PART I.
FIRST
WARNING.

things at the same moment. Such a physical obstacle might scarcely hold in the spiritual service of the Christian's will. There is a deeper moral obstacle on which Jesus fastens our attention. Man's moral service does not rest, like a slave's, on compulsion, but on choice. It is determined by the likings of the man. And where two rival moral masters are issuing contrary behests, it is simply out of the question that his own inclination should fall in with the will of both. He must either like what A prescribes, and in that event he will hate B for prescribing the opposite; or else, on the other hand, if he cleave by preference to the orders of B, he must practically despise or set aside the authority of A.[1]

Thus, then, the case stands with a christian disciple who is falling under the sway of covetousness. He must in the end renounce entirely the service of God, and become in soul and will the very bond-slave of money. By choosing here an unusual Chaldee word for wealth, Jesus has marked a little more firmly His personification of all worldly property as wielding a power over men antagonistic to the authority of God Him-

mamonas.

---

[1] I have taken the liberty of following (with Alford, *in loc.*) Meyer's ingenious and simple way of representing the dual alternative of v. 24 by letters. See his Commentary.

self. But so bold a personification can mislead no one. That money is a hard master has been the testimony of multitudes, who, after slaving all their days to get it, cursed it at last in the bitterness of death for a worthless cheat. But money has no mastership save over him who loves it. It sways men by their hearts. It comes at last, if you will let it, not simply to divide your allegiance with God Himself, but to detach you from God's household altogether, and reduce you to a slavery which degrades you. Such abject slavery to gold, however, is the miserable issue of a downward progress. It began when the man began to heap up for himself treasures upon earth. It laid the foundation of its power, when it seduced the man's heart, and drew down his love from heaven to earth. It has detached him from its heavenly rival and secured him for its own, by putting out his eyes that he should no longer see the better wealth of eternity. And now, it alone fills his narrowed vision; it alone is loved by his earthly heart; and because gold he will have, and gold he takes joy in, therefore is he become a willing servant to his own covetousness, a worshipper and a slave of mammon.

Let no one ask how that can be called bondage which a man does because he likes to do it. For

PART I.

FIRST WARNING.

Ver. 19.

Ver. 21.

Ver. 22.

PART I.
FIRST WARNING.

it is precisely here, in the fettering of any one's heart to a base or insufficient thing, in the subjugation of his higher nobler self, his reason, his conscience, and his love, to something which was made to be his servant, not his master, that moral slavery, the only slavery which reaches or degrades the man himself, must be sought for.

Lovelace: From Prison.

'Stone walls do not a prison make,
Nor iron bars a cage :'

as little can the manacle on the wrist or the lash on the shoulder make a slave. But when a man's own pride sways him against his reason, or lust proves stronger than temperate resolution, or the foolish longing to be soon rich drags a soul after

Cf. 1 Tim. vi. 9.

it to perdition, in defiance of wisdom and of piety; then it is the very man himself who is yoked to the car of his own vices, and taken captive in a

John viii. 34, Greek.

most base, because a willing captivity. 'Every one that doeth sin is a slave of the sin.' And the test of such slavery lies in this, that he is no longer able to do the will of God. Against the structure of their own moral nature, people are continually flattering themselves that it is possible to live in a divided allegiance. It is possible, to be sure, that for a moment of indecision, while two opposite impulses stand in conflict, a man may hover betwixt the two. But no man can

Against Covetousness. 43

live so. His own choice decides his service. He gives himself to the work which he likes best. He cannot do that, and also give himself to opposite work which he likes less. Still less can he continue to do that, and yet retain the power of giving himself to its opposite. It is not the will only, but the whole nature of a man, from the heart outwards, which gets so wedded to the service to which he has once devoted his strength, that it comes to be in the long-run a thing inconceivable by him, and utterly unattainable, that he should transfer to any novel master the settled labour of his life.

PART I.

FIRST WARNING.

This is the abyss to which Jesus points His followers, that they may shun the beginnings of the incline. In this world His kingdom must be ; and by the gains of this world His servants must live ; and the hand of diligent Christians will make rich. But in such incessant contact with wealth and acquisition of it, the eye of our King foresaw an incessant peril. How serious that peril proved to be to the Church after she outgrew persecution, and began to suck the wealth of kingdoms, may be read in a whole millennium of Western Church history. How great it has always proved to the individual Christian, may

Prov. x. 4.

PART I.
FIRST
WARNING.

be seen on every hand of us at this hour. There is no safeguard but to follow with fearful and averted faces the warning of our King: 'Lay not up for yourselves treasures upon earth.' All needless superfluous storing—storing for vanity, not for prudence, for delight, not for use — is pregnant with spiritual danger. Scatter your treasures rather; buy heavenly friends with earthly mammon; sell and give alms; for though the little heap may be but small, experience warns us that it can steal the heart. And when a heart which ought to have its eye on God, its home above, its wealth in eternity, has been allured to settle on its heap of gold, alas for the blinding of the eyes and the enslaving of the will! How great is that darkness! How hopeless that captivity!

Luke xvi. 9.

AGAINST ANXIETY.

Therefore I say unto you, Take no thought for your life, what ye shall eat, or what ye shall drink: nor yet for your body, what ye shall put on. Is not the life more than meat, and the body than raiment? Behold the fowls of the air: for they sow not, neither do they reap, nor gather into barns; yet your heavenly Father feedeth them. Are ye not much better than they? Which of you, by taking thought, can add one cubit to his stature? And why take ye thought for raiment? Consider the lilies of the field, how they grow; they toil not, neither do they spin: and yet I say unto you, That even Solomon, in all his glory, was not arrayed like one of these. Wherefore, if God so clothe the grass of the field, which to-day is, and to-morrow is cast into the oven, shall He not much more clothe you, O ye of little faith? Therefore take no thought, saying, 'What shall we eat?' or, 'What shall we drink?' or, 'Wherewithal shall we be clothed?' For after all these things do the Gentiles seek: for your heavenly Father knoweth that ye have need of all these things. But seek ye first the kingdom of God and His righteousness; and all these things shall be added unto you. Take therefore no thought for the morrow; for the morrow shall take thought for the things of itself. Sufficient unto the day is the evil thereof.—MATT. VI. 25–34; cf. LUKE XII. 22–32.

AGAINST ANXIETY.

COVETOUSNESS is the temptation which lies nearest to persons whose worldly fortune is sufficient for their need, and believed to be safe or assured; anxiety, that which besets all those whose means are either uncertain or insufficient. This division does not exactly coincide either with that between wealth and poverty, as we commonly use these terms, or with the distinction between a narrow and an easy income: for in the humbler classes of society, a man in good health may be sufficiently raised above fear of want to stand in greater danger of making even his slender gains a treasure, than of any anxiety about his future; whereas there are plenty of opulent business men whose capital, ample as it is, is exposed to such incessant hazard through the speculations of trade, that so far from resting in the joy of possession, they live unhappy days through the apprehension of loss. To be raised above this new foe—anxiety—one's income must in the first place be at least adequate to meet without strain that expenditure, be it great or little, which has become necessary to one's happiness; and in the next place, there must be a fair prospect that it will continue to meet it. It does not depend on the amount a man has, but on the proportion between what he has and what he desires to spend, together with the security with which he believes he may count upon a similar proportion in the future. When, therefore, we have discounted all persons in any position of life who are reasonably assured of continuing to have enough for their requirements, we shall find that we have set aside only the fortunate and envied few, and that we have still to reckon with the vast bulk of mankind, rich or poor, on whom sits a dismal comrade, a black shadow, whose name is Care.

It is true indeed that covetousness itself, even before it has reached its full limit and become the confirmed moral disease which we term avarice, is a prolific mother of cares. Wealth has its anxieties as well as poverty; and the cares of the wealthy are far less excusable than those of the poor. There even comes a point in the growth of a soul's bondage to money at which its delight in what it possesses becomes feebler than the torturing fear of losing it; and then

PART I.
SECOND WARNING.

Atra cura: Horace.

Against Anxiety. 49

ensues the shocking spectacle, so often pictured by the moralist and the literary artist, of a human being consumed with the incessant alarms and the sordid anxieties of penury in the very midst of unused money-bags. But this appears to me to be only a vivid, because an extreme, illustration of the profound spiritual affinity which subsists betwixt these two sore abuses of worldly substance. Though contrasted in their surface manifestations and besetting opposite social classes, these two— idolatrous delight in possession, and faithless fear for want—are yet at bottom kindred vices. Trace them to their root; and you find that they spring from the same religious apostasy,—a preference of the earthly before the spiritual, of what this life can give before the rewards of our heavenly Father. Indeed, I take it to be a note, pointing us to this inner kinship betwixt the two, when our Lord passes from the first of them to the second with the word 'Therefore.'[1] Because the diversion of one's supreme affection from celestial and future rewards to settle on the treasures of earth, leads to such disastrous spiritual results as blindness to the divine and slavery to mammon, Cf. vers. 21-24.

PART I.
SECOND WARNING.

διὰ ταῦτα, ver. 25.

---

[1] The parallel passage in St. Luke (xii. 22-32) actually occurs in connection with a warning, not against anxiety, but against 'covetousness.' Cf. ver. 15 of that chapter.

D

PART I.
SECOND
WARNING.

'therefore' avoid it in every shape; not only in that shape of covetous idolatry which leads men to amass wealth and delight themselves in its possession, but not less also in that still more frequent shape of carking care which frets one's days by a disquieting apprehension of want. For this, too, is a sort of bondage to money; this, too, shows that the eye for divine things has been darkened; this, not less than the other, springs from, and in its turn confirms, the degradation of the heart to rest upon treasures that are perishable.

The whole force, then, of such considerations as Jesus has already urged in support of His first admonition to 'treasure no treasures,' is transferred by this connecting word 'therefore,' to enforce His second admonition as well: 'Take no anxious thought.' At the same time, every one must be struck by the different tone which marks His address to the anxious-minded. What He says to them, indeed, is not less urgent, or insistant, than what has been said to the covetous; yet it is mixed with a certain unmistakeable gentleness, and passes almost insensibly from expostulation into words of comfort. To the rich, who prided themselves on riches and were greedy for more, Jesus spoke with a severity which, in

Against Anxiety. 51

its hard exposure of gold's darkening and enslaving influence, bordered upon threatening. To the poor who toil for to-day's bread, and are fearful of to-morrow's hunger, He speaks with a kindliness which does not border upon promising, but abounds in it. He bids them be confident; He reasons down their fears; He cheers them by the liberal bounty of Providence to flower and bird; He repeats expostulations with a sweet persuasiveness; He does everything to encourage them to a more generous confidence in their heavenly Father. There is good reason for this. Such slavery to the perishing gains of earth as grows out of one's treasured abundance is a vice of the lofty, the idle, the prosperous, and the pampered classes. It is a 'superfluity of naughtiness.' It is bred of the misdirected pride and misused delights of mankind. It deserves little sympathy, and needs no encouragement. Whereas such care as comes to knit the forehead of earth's hard-pressed toilers and darken all their hours with fear of want, is born of the feebleness and joylessness of our curse. It is the portion of the lowly, the unfortunate, and the poor. It argues infirmity, not pride, in us; and is best cured by the sympathy of a Son Who became poor, and the encouragements of a Father Who cares for His

PART I.

SECOND
WARNING.

Jas. i. 21.

little ones. It was quite in the temper of the older prophets of His people, that Jesus of Nazareth thus changed His tone to mildness when He turned from the covetous rich to the careworn poor; and we may be sure that, in this as in all things, He faithfully reflected the mind of the Father above. But from His lips such a change of tone wore a special propriety. Mary's Son was a poor man from the day of His birth to the day of His death. The eldest-born of an artisan's widow, early experience had made Him familiar with the narrow resources of poor people and their shifty economy, often on the brink of straitness whenever disease comes to cripple the working hand, or fear of death is made bitterer by the fear of penury. Since He abandoned Nazareth for an itinerant life, He had already begun to taste the trials of a still more hand-to-mouth dependence upon Heaven for daily bread, and the emergencies of one who subsists upon the chance offerings of friendship, and knows not sometimes where to lay his head. Granting that the glitter of Judea's crown was cast once or twice across His path with sufficient clearness to make Him understand what fascination an earthly treasure may have for the few; still it was out of a more habitual fellow-feeling He could turn to the hard-worked and ill-paid thousands of His countrymen, and bid them trust their heavenly Father for daily food. He surely knows to this hour how bitter a trial it is for any honest labouring man, to see his small savings wear done while the hands which ought to be toiling lie white and wasting on the coverlid; to watch the decent raiment of wife and little ones turn tattered with no hope of new, and the tiny face that was pale before grow punier and more pale day by day; to miss one little article after another from the room, and say nothing, but let the hidden dread of destitution gnaw the sick heart with silent misery. When He bids such a man trust God, He surely means no mockery, but effectual help. Jesus of Nazareth was and is the poor man's best friend; nor have any words been ever spoken on this earth better suited to the lot of the toiling masses, or so brimful of real, wise, effectual sustaining strength for faint-hearted humanity in its mean and every-day necessities, as these blessed words of Jesus.

Let us first try to fix what that fault precisely is, which Jesus has here chidden with such gentle urgency. Everything will depend on the sense which we affix to one word only; for although

PART I.
SECOND
WARNING.
μεριμνᾶν, vers.
25, 31, 34.

'Take no thought.'

our Lord has repeated His exhortation no fewer than three times, He has adhered in every instance to the use of the same verb. The rendering of that verb consistently followed by our version is, to our ears at least, so weak as really to misrepresent the sense. To 'take thought' about any matter, means in ordinary English little more than to exercise one's mind respecting it, so as to do the best that can be done under the circumstances to avoid complications or to bring about a desirable issue. This is not only not what Jesus means to prohibit, it is almost exactly the reverse of it. For such calm, judicious exercise both of thought and of forethought regarding worldly provision as will lead to diligent and successful endeavours to secure it, is not only a different thing from the state of anxiety censured by our Lord, but is really inconsistent with it. In fact, it is one of the minor objections to over-anxiety,[1] that it disturbs the judgment, and makes one's endeavours inconstant and ineffectual. It is really a foe to such calm consideration and deliberate action as must always be the duty of an intelligent human being placed in a world of labour, and weighted with the responsibility of

---

[1] μεριμνᾶν, from μερίζω, implies the division or distraction of the mind among a variety of opposite contingencies.

Against Anxiety. 55

providing for his own and his dependants' subsistence. Even the word 'care' (or 'have care,' or 'be careful'), substituted in other passages where the same Greek verb occurs in the same sense, fails to express the thought. To 'care for' anything is an ambiguous phrase; used sometimes indeed to describe a fault, but sometimes also to describe a virtue. We have no choice open to us better than to read it thus: 'Be not anxious about your life.' Though 'anxiety' may in certain cases carry no suspicion of blame with it, yet by its etymology[1] it always involves a degree of concern which is so overstrained or excessive as to have become painful. The state of mind really described by our Lord's words is such solicitude about future events or issues against which we have no resource, as divides and distracts and fruitlessly distresses the mind, so as to destroy its peace.[2] It only begins, therefore, at the point where rational and dutiful carefulness ends. When a man, set in the thick of life, with a crowd of possibilities swarming about his path, any one of which might, if it became actual, ruin his fortune or starve his family, can keep his head cool enough

PART I.

SECOND WARNING.
Cf. Luke x. 41; 1 Cor. vii. 32–34, xii. 25; Phil. ii. 20, iv. 6; 1 Pet. v. 7.

[1] From Latin *angere*. Cf. *anguish*, and the same root in Germ. Eng., etc.
[2] μεριμνᾶν est ita curare ut sollicitus sis ne res defutura sit in tempore. Tittmann, *de Synonymis*, p. 137.

PART I.
SECOND
WARNING.

to think out, and his hand steady enough to work through, whatever it lies in his power, guided by foresight, to do; he has reached the point at which his own duty ends, and the unknown dispensations of Providence enter. At that point reason and piety alike enjoin that solicitude should be arrested, and that trust should take its place. Reason condemns further solicitude regarding that which no thoughtfulness or care of ours can affect, as useless; piety rebukes it as distrustful. The reward which is to crown human industry or forethought is to be of God's bestowing; the incidence upon individual history of those numberless events which men call accidental, because they cannot forecast them, must lie in God's hand; the region of the future, like that of the unknown, is His; and the office of an intelligent faith is humbly to wait on Him for the fruits of past labour and the falling out of our lot.

It is distrust of God, therefore, which lies at the root of unlawful anxiety. A feeble apprehension of God, as the Agent Who overrules everything, and determines those causes which lie outside of our reach and those events which escape our foresight; this it is which shakes the soul with vague uncertainty, and fills with causeless alarms the darkness of to-morrow. The doubt whether God, Who counts for so much in the contingencies of life, be One Whose attitude to us may be wholly trusted, or the suspicion that we may have really as much to dread as to hope for from His superintendence; this it is which cannot but unsettle a man's stedfast outlook into the coming days, and toss his spirit to and fro in the restlessness of distraction. Because we are 'of little faith,' therefore are we not content to plan and work, and having planned and wrought, to sit and wait; but must fidget ourselves about that which may be, until impatience gnaws us like a worm, and our imagination, picturing disasters in the dark, burns us like fire. Why is it that popular proverbs attest how much worse are fancied ills than real ones, and how the evils which we most dread never overtake us; but just because this distrustful human heart of ours is so prone to prophesy, and so lively to exaggerate, misfortune? Like a soothing, cooling breath from a serener world, there comes down upon the feverish, self-tormenting spirits of men this word of One Who was the messenger of Him Whom we distrust: 'Be not anxious about your life: be not anxious about to-morrow!'

Distrustful anxiety, in the sense now explained, is far from being confined to any single

PART I.
SECOND WARNING.

Ver. 30.

PART I.
SECOND
WARNING.

set of human circumstances. Just as the human heart may make a treasure to itself of any precious thing as well as of money, so men may indulge a sinful solicitude respecting any other apprehended calamity as well as destitution. Again, therefore, the spirit of our Lord's words goes far beyond their immediate and literal scope. A timid or desponding nature is constitutionally prone to expect the worst; it peoples to-morrow with its fears, and lives under the shadow of what may never be; while just in proportion as our love has learned to prize and live upon any treasured possession, will its instinct be quick to divine the approach of that which threatens to rob us of it. What is so jealous of loss as love? or seems to itself to stand more continually in jeopardy? But just as, in the preceding half of this paragraph, superfluous riches stood for all such objects of delight rather than of need as men are ready to store up for their pride; so here the simplest provision for bodily wants is put for whatever men conceive to be indispensable to life,—that is to say, for whatever ministers, not to superfluous delight, but to absolute necessity. The 'life' for which Jesus entreats us to take no anxious thought, is that life whose primary requirements are food and raiment; not as if the most elementary conception of our physical and social existence in a civilised state did not include a multitude of other *desiderata*, nearly, if not quite, as indispensable as even these; but only because in these you have the earliest and typical examples of what earth must yield to man, if his life on earth is to be maintained. With that large class of our fellow-creatures to whom life has become in the strictest sense a struggle for the means of subsistence, the questions which before every other press for instant reply are just such questions as Jesus has here put into the mouth of the anxious: 'What shall we eat? what shall we drink? wherewithal shall we be clothed?' And however far we may be placed above the risk of literal starvation, we shall hardly be able to excuse our excessive apprehensions for the future, unless we can plead that the things we fear to be deprived of deserve to be ranked by us in the same imperative category with meat and drink and raiment. It is true that there are other necessities which do deserve to be ranked with these—necessities not all of them of a material kind. Even as an earthly creature, 'man doth not live by bread only.' The deeper hunger of the intellect for knowledge may crave as imperiously as the bodily appetite. Strip a human soul of all re-

PART I.

SECOND WARNING.

Cf. μεριμναις βιωτικαις in Luke xxi. 34.

Deut. viii. 3, quoted Matt. iv. 4.

Cf. Amos viii. 11.

PART I.
SECOND
WARNING.

spectful or compassionate fellowship from his fellows, and you leave him to the stony loveless stare of society and the inclemencies of fortune, in a nakedness more to be pitied than that of the body. To be threatened with such loss as that s literally to be in anxiety for one's life, even though bread and water may not fail. But surely it were quite enough to put to shame the myriad ignoble and paltry anxieties with which our easy lives are daily vexed, to ask: Are these, then, matters of so great moment to our 'life,' that to want them, though we should want them for ever, would be to us like the extremity of hunger or the shame of nakedness?

Vers. 25-34.

Our Lord has been careful to enforce His warning against anxiety about the means of living by a variety of arguments, partly addressed to reason and partly to piety: drawn, too, in part from the lessons of nature, and in part from the Kingdom of Heaven. The whole passage thus becomes a precious specimen of the harmony which unites the teachings of God in His natural creation with those of His christian revelation; a specimen the more precious, that it comes from His lips Who is the Author of both. This speaker Who finds in God's natural providence the same lesson which Christians have more plainly learnt through the revelation of our Father's grace, is that very Word, or expression of the Godhead, by Whom in the beginning all things were made, and by Whom also in the end of the world we have been given to know the Father. Of nature He speaks as its Framer; of the gospel as its Revealer: and the one mighty lesson—cure for all sordid cares—in which He finds the voices of nature and revelation to unite, is that God's providence on man's behalf is absolutely to be trusted. In nature it is God as our Maker Whom we come to know, and what as our Maker He may be expected to do for such creatures as we are. In the gospel kingdom, we find God to be more than Maker, a Father in heaven; and receive a measure by which to estimate how much as a Father He is likely to do for His children. But the two discoveries coincide. The Framer of nature is 'a faithful Creator,' into Whose hands His human creatures may safely 'commit the keeping of their lives' in well-doing. The Revealer of the gospel is a tender Father, Who, not having 'spared His Son' for us, 'will with Him also freely give us all things.' The meeting-point of the two teachings lies in the personal trustworthiness of God as the provider

PART I.

SECOND WARNING.

John i. 1–3; Heb. i. 2, 3.

Cf. 1 Pet. iv. 19, where ψυχας has the double sense of 'souls' or 'lives.'

Rom. viii. 32.

for man's life. As the cure for covetousness was found in an eager and satisfying delight in God as the present treasure of our souls, leading to a hopeful anticipation of His rewards in the remoter and eternal future; so the cure for anxiety is found in a childlike confidence upon God as the author and maintainer of our life, leading to a most restful expectation that He will provide for us in the near and earthly to-morrow. We have seen that the parent of all culpable anxiety about the future is named 'Little-faith.' It is eminently a heathenish sin, of which christian people ought to be ashamed; although even the heathen might learn enough from the fowls of the air and the flowers of the field to save them from seeking after their daily bread under the burden of a painful fear lest they should never find it, as though they had been sent into this world like uncared-for foundlings, or the step-children of niggardly and partial Nature. Heaven's bounty to the meanest thing that lives rebukes the distrust even of the pagan. How much greater cause have we, who know ourselves to be in the kingdom of our heavenly Father, to leave on His charge, with a generous abandonment, the care of our bodily requirements, while we devote ourselves with supreme concern to the accomplishment of His will, and the practical establishment of His sovereignty!

PART I.
SECOND WARNING.

I. The first class of dissuasives from anxiety are those which are drawn from reason and the natural dealings of God with His creation.

(1.) Of these the first is given in these words: 'Is not the life more than meat, and the body than raiment?' It is an argument from the greater to the less; from the end to the means for that end. Food and raiment are not ends in themselves; they become needful to man only for the sake of that physical life which, if unfed, must cease, and that material body whose natural condition is one of imperfect protection. But this body, made so wonderfully, yet left so undefended, and this life that cannot live without assistance from the vegetable and animal creation, are not of our own making or getting. They are God's unsolicited gifts, wrought by His skilful workmanship, and quickened, no man can discover how, by the secret might of His will. The author of so strange and precious a piece of mechanism as this living body may be trusted to care for His own handiwork. Since He must mean that the covering which He has denied to it by nature shall be supplied by human art, He will not with-

Ver. 25.

Cf. Ps. cxxxix. 14–16.

hold the material for garments, nor fail to bless the spinner and the weaver. If it is by bread we are to sustain life, then He Who gave the life will help us to sow the seed and reap the grain. It cannot be the purpose of our Maker that His pains in making us what we are should fail of their design through want of such minor aids and ministers to existence as our state requires. To feed and clothe, is a less thing than to make, a human being. On our side, therefore, our dependence on God for existence warrants our trusting Him for subsistence; since, on God's part, His having cared to create us at all is a pledge that He will take care to provide for us. To reason thus concerning God, is to take for granted that the analogy of human action is in such a case a safe guide to the discovery of the divine. It proceeds on the assumption that, as men, if they are wise, will not do a great deal for any end, and then refuse to do the little more which that end requires, so neither will He Who made men. Jesus not only confirms such reasoning as just, but implies that reasoning like this ought always to have saved the multitude of the poor from distrustful solicitude about the means of living.

(2.) Such an à *priori* inference, our Lord argues

in the second place, is very abundantly confirmed by our observation of inferior nature. What we may conclude beforehand that it would be reasonable in our Maker to do for us, is just what we find Him doing for other creatures. Man is part of a larger whole; a fellow-denizen of this fair earth with a multitude of less noble inhabitants. His physical frame, which needs to be fed and clothed, is precisely that which links him so closely to the rest of the material creation, as to make him, though its ruling member, yet a true member of it, subject, like other organisms, to its laws of growth, support, and decay. He Who made man a material creature, in need of nutriment for his life and decorous covering for his body, made also those other organized creatures with which he shares such mean necessities in common. If they, acting after their kind, are neither abandoned nor neglected by their Maker, why should he alone be suffered to want? Nay, far less will he be suffered. By how much man excels other animals through the higher development of his nature and the dignity of his station upon earth, above all by that distinguishing image of his Creator which links him to the spiritual and divine; by so much the rather is it to be presumed that God, Who leaves no humbler thing

PART I.

SECOND WARNING.

E

The Relations of the Kingdom.

PART I.
SECOND WARNING.
Cf. Ps. viii.

untended, will care for His princely and surpassing creature, on whose head there rests the crown of terrestrial creation.

Ver. 26.

This mode of reasoning is put with homely concreteness. A teacher sitting out of doors in Palestine in a populous neighbourhood, would seldom be able to point to any undomesticated animals within sight, except birds; and of course domesticated animals, for which man provides, could not be so fitly adduced in proof of God's direct care for His creatures. But of 'fowls of the air' there could never be any lack. Not to

Luke xii. 24.

speak of the raven, which, on a parallel occasion in St. Luke, our Lord specially named, it is well known that flocks of pigeons, field-sparrows, and other small birds are everywhere to be found in Palestine, to-day, as well as in Bible times. To these light wanderers of the air, therefore, as they flew past on careless wing in search of food, Jesus directed His audience with peculiar felicity. These offered the best example of a creature for whose wants man does not care, and which no instinct of its own teaches to lay up any store, which lives in fact from day to day on the casual bounty of nature, yet lives of all creatures the freest and lightest-hearted life. The swallow chatters on the wing while it chases its food, as though it were to be always summer. The lark shakes rapture from his throat in such abandonment of glee, as if men beneath were never full of care. Why not? He Whose eye rests on their lowly loves, forages for their frugal meal. Summer by summer, God hangs on every hedgerow and wild bramble bush an ample store of berries by which, through severe dead months, the field-birds are to be kept from starving. Autumn by autumn, He sends them to glean the leavings of man's harvest-field. No sowing or reaping has He asked from them; not even such garnering as He has taught to the squirrel and the ant; but will keep them in close dependence on the provision of His own hand, set forth on His large earth-table, ready for their picking. That which He giveth them, they gather. The gathering of it, as they need it, is all that is in their care; except, indeed, the glad song of thanks which the full heart of the little creature trills on the spray when the meal is done. These field-birds are but specimens indeed, but they are very near and touching and vocal specimens, of that wide family of unlabouring and careless creatures, which in earth and sky and sea 'seeks' everywhere 'its meat from God.' When one comes to think of it, it seems surprising how rarely, under ordinary circumstances, any

PART I.

SECOND WARNING.

Ps. civ. 28.

Said of the young lions in Ps. civ. 21. Cf. of the ravens in Job xxxviii. 41.

PART I.
SECOND
WARNING.

Luke xv. 17.

Ver. 28.

of the wilder beasts are found to starve. Earth is full of competing life; and the history of the animals which crowd and swarm and prey upon each other is but a 'struggle for existence.' Yet, under the adjustments of divine law, that which they seek, they do for the most part find; and live out their appointed time, careless of to-morrow, yet secure of food for to-morrow's hunger. The meanest servant in our Father's house has 'bread enough and to spare.' 'Are ye not much better than they?'

'And why take ye thought for raiment?' If it was in the time of spring that our Lord discoursed this Sermon, the fields around Him would be gay with the numerous wild-flowers of Syria, and the hill-side grass on which His hearers reclined might offer to His hand the lesson of the lilies. Science has failed as yet to fix for us the exact species of lily to which Jesus pointed as more gorgeous than an oriental monarch's robe;[1]

---

[1] The reign of Solomon was in all outward prosperity by far the most memorable which Hebrew annals could boast. It was, in fact, the only time at which the little Hebrew state could claim to be the centre of an empire on the oriental scale; and the magnificence of that opulent and splendour-loving monarch so impressed the national imagination, that it continued to stand for a type of all earthly greatness. See the inspired account in 2 Chron. ix. 13-28; and compare Rawlinson, *Anc. Mon.* ii. 80, with note, and Ewald, *Gesch. d. Volkes Israel*, B. iii.

but the wild-flowering plants of His land, like those of our own, are rich enough in lovely hues and tender texture to furnish us with more than one example of His general lesson. They grow up among the lowly pastures; they hide themselves beneath the budding woods; they mix with the neglected spikes of flowering grasses by the wayside. To be trodden under foot, or cut down in a timberless land for fuel to feed the domestic oven, is their most frequent fate; while the best fortune they dare hope for is only to be plucked by the fickle hand of childhood, toyed with for an hour, then flung aside for their too speedy withering. These are not the costly products of cultivation, which lend themselves to deck the saloons or share the revels of the wealthy; these stand, in the prodigality of God, where the husbandman plies his scythe and beside the poor man's cottage door. Yet not the meanest of them all but is clad in raiment fit for a king; nay, their soft petals are woven with a fineness of fibre and closeness of transparent texture such as no loom can rival, in tints whose delicacy and purity surpass the dyes of Tyre. For the dress of man, being artificial and his own, can be nothing more than borrowed as to its material, and imitated as to its colouring; borrowed from the plant's

PART I.
SECOND
WARNING.

Gen. iii. 7.

stem or from the worm's cocoon; imitated from the radiant colours which gleam upon the wood-bird's breast, or glow among the grass in the wild-flower's crown of splendour. The garments which men need for their shame, they are fain to decorate for their pride. To be clothed is not enough; they must be clothed in gay attire. Yet, when they have done their utmost, they only strive, but strive in vain, to emulate that profuse and fairer loveliness which God has scattered over His whole creation. 'Consider' this; watch the silent growth of lilies, so unlike the clash and hurry of man's spinning factory; and as each one uprears its tender stem of green, and unfolds above its glorious coronet of purple or of gold, think whether He Who cares to make so fair the grass of the field that blossoms for a day, may not be trusted to drape in needful garments the unsheltered and ashamed flesh of His immortal child!

Such a generous confidence in the providential care of God for to-morrow's provision both of food and of clothing, rests as a matter of course on our own diligence and careful prudence to-day. To act as if we were fowls or lilies, and needed as little as they to sow and spin, would be no less insolent than preposterous. It is only after God's noblest creature and proper child has done all that lies in the child's part to do, according to his constitution and place in creation,—has sown his field where the birds are picking up their portion from the furrow, and woven his garment in imitation of the splendour of lilies,—that man, the sower and the reaper and the spinner, comes to stand in the same position of immediate dependence upon the care of God which the lower creatures occupy. By nature he is a provident animal; they improvident by nature. It is the privilege of his nobility that he can be, up to a given point, a fellow-worker with God in that needful toil, and in that moral forethoughtfulness, and even in that artistic skill, by which creature existence is both sustained and adorned. Here, therefore, and up to this point, every true child who prizes his place of fellowship with the Father, will work where the Father has wrought before him and still is working with him. All effective profitable labour of man, whether for use or for beauty,—for the culture of the soil or the decoration of the robe,—rests on a child-like comprehension first, and then a child-like imitation, of the works of God. We are the students and the coadjutors of the Divine Worker in those natural processes by which His earth is made to minister to its inhabitants; and we can have no right to

PART I.
SECOND
WARNING.

expect that He Who invites the attention of our intellect and the aid of our hand, will do for His heedless or slothful children what they will not do for themselves. But when the human faculties have been fairly employed in their legitimate sphere, and man has striven, as he could, to enter into this honourable place assigned him as his distinction over inferior creatures, is it to be thought that He Who caters for the birds and clothes the grass, will forget to bless the labour, or refuse to provide for the wants, of one whom He has associated with Himself in a nobler fellowship of intelligence and of toil?

Before I pass from this exquisite appeal to the providence of God in His inferior creation, I cannot but notice how significant it is of our Lord's eye for nature. In contrast to ancient systems of nature-worship, it was characteristic first of Judaism and then of Christianity, that they fastened attention on the exceptional dignity of man as the only moral and immortal creature upon earth, on sin as the supreme fact in human experience, and on the rectification of our spiritual relations with God as our supreme need. In Christianity especially, the salvation of the soul becomes the one thing of transcendent moment in man's earthly existence. It is not wonderful that the effect of

Luke x. 42.

such teaching was at first, and has often been, to quench the delight of Christians in natural beauty, to discourage science as a waste of time and art as a vain idolatry, and to lead devout minds to feel as if nothing else on earth deserved a moment's thought save the eternal interests of man himself. How little countenance any such unnatural or one-sided excess of religious earnestness derives from our Master, this present passage is enough to teach us.[1] The interests of human spirits could not but be the one matter on earth of supreme consequence to Him Who had come to earth on purpose to ransom them; yet His spirit was so healthily balanced, that He could spare time and thought not only for men's bodies, but even for the inferior animals. To note the habits of the birds, and watch with kindly eye their happy carelessness upon the wing, was a portion of His duty and delight Who walked His Father's earth as the Son of God; and it was not a forgotten portion. When science shall have learnt to observe and examine nature in the same spirit of child-like joy in God, in hope to draw from its researches a profounder and more intelligent ac-

PART I.

SECOND
WARNING.

Cf. for example, John iv. 31–34.

[1] Our Lord's close observation of nature and delight in it may be inferred from such incidental notices in the Gospels as the following: Matt. xvi. 2; Luke xii. 54; Matt. xxiv. 32; John xv. 1–6; Matt. xxiii. 37, xxvi. 34; and others.

quaintance with the thoughts of God, on which to rear a more perfect trust in Him, science will be accomplishing its highest function. But it will then walk in the footsteps of Christ; by patient investigation and in exacter methods following up the hint which is really offered to us by His popular interpretations of nature. It is quite the same with art. The moral and religious regeneration of mankind was the task which consumed the labours and drunk up the spirit of our Master; yet He could pause on His way to admire the colour of a lily. The law which regulates all decorative art is, that it shall apply to the adornment of whatever is required for human convenience, such principles of beauty in form and colour as have been reached by the study of beauty in nature. This is just the law which underlies our Lord's comparison and preference of the flower to the royal robe; while the evident love He has for the simple loveliness of form and colour in a wild-flower is precisely the root out of which all great art has ever sprung. A docile and delighted affection for the workmanship of God's hand, is in truth the christian attitude to every natural phenomenon. Out of this root it is that these fair twin growths come forth: the study of natural facts and laws, so that from what He does we may learn what God thinks, which is science; and the study of natural beauty, so that from what He has done joyfully, we may learn what God admires, which is art.

PART I.

SECOND WARNING.

(3.) For convenience' sake, I have treated together the lessons of the bird and of the lily; but between these two our Teacher interjects a third argument to show the unreasonableness of anxiety. Perhaps it is inserted immediately after the lesson of the fowls which God feeds, just because it attaches itself to the idea of food rather than to that of clothing. But the question, 'Which of you, by taking thought, can add one cubit unto his stature?' covers what is really a new argument. What that argument is, comes out quite clearly from the words (awanting in St. Matthew) with which St. Luke, in a parallel place, continues the reasoning: 'If ye then be not able to do that thing which is least, why take ye thought for the rest?' What, then, is this 'least thing' which no one can do? The words of our English version suggest of themselves some suspicion of error in the rendering; for, to add a 'cubit' (which can hardly mean less than a foot and a half[1]) to the height of a man would be so far from a 'least' thing, that it would be an enor-

Ver. 27.

Luke xii. 26.

ἐλάχιστον.

---

[1] Some uncertainty obtains as to the longer and shorter

mous and unheard of thing. The word our Lord uses, however, means strictly the period of life when a man is at his maturity; embracing, of course, the two connected ideas of the years he has lived and the physical development he has attained. In at least one passage of the Gospels, it carries this sense. Here we are certainly guided by the connection to the idea of age or period of life, rather than to that of height or personal stature. It is of the food by which life is prolonged Jesus has been speaking; not yet of the body, its stature or its dress. And though the use of the word 'cubit' in relation even to the length of one's life sounds in our ears a little harsh, it is really quite as natural a metaphor as when David sighs: 'Thou hast made my days as an handbreadth.' So read, the reasoning becomes at least intelligible. Experience teaches that such anxiety as Jesus reproves is a useless thing. To what serves all our fretting and fidgeting over the future, when we cannot so much as prolong by the least bit the measure of our own days, or the

margin notes: PART I. SECOND WARNING. ἡλικία. John ix. 21, 23.[1] Ps. xxxix. 5.

scriptural measures known under this name, and their exact lengths. See art. in Smith's *Dict.*, 'Weights and Measures.'

[1] On the other hand, it certainly means 'stature' in Luke xix. 3; probably also in ii. 52. In Heb. xi. 11 it undoubtedly has the sense of 'the child-bearing period of life;' and in Eph. iv. 13 it may possibly be 'full manhood' (as the age of military service ?).

Against Anxiety. 77

period of manhood's unbroken strength? You fear for coming years; but no carefulness on your part can so much as secure that you shall live to see them. You would fain control beforehand those myriad influences of nature and of human fortune which threaten beforehand to overwhelm your life with calamity; how vain a craving in a creature so impotent that, were all the resources of nature, together with every human assistance, at your command, you could not avert by one hour the disabling stroke of sickness or the fatal shaft of death! Why need men vex themselves in vain over the great and far-off things of the world's providence and of its future, since so near and small a matter as their own fragile existence is from moment to moment suspended upon the will of Another? So long as he is content to move within the narrow room allowed him, man can do something to help himself; but it is by respecting those bars of creature limitation which so closely fence him in, not by dashing his feebleness against their iron strength.

PART I.
SECOND WARNING.

II. Thus by argument after argument, open all of them to the eye of natural reason, did the Son of God intend His earthly works and providence to persuade men to live dependent lives, confiding

PART I.
SECOND
WARNING.

in their Creator's bounty. Thus from the first it had been a lesson of creation that He Who made us living men might be trusted to care for the perishable life He has kindled in our frames; and a lesson of providence, which lets no creature want, that much less shall we be left without any Eye to oversee or any Hand to provide for us; and a lesson of our own daily experience that anxiety is futile, since we are impotent to control events, or so much as secure for ourselves one hour of lusty life. But, forasmuch as these voices of nature had proved too low to be caught, or too inarticulate to be understood, or too unwelcome to be remembered; so that, in point of fact, the nations of mankind had not been preserved from the most distressing and faithless anxiety in their struggle for existence: therefore is the Son of God come down to interpret into human speech these unheard or unheeded lessons; and not to rehearse them only in our hearing, but to add to them the far more cogent persuasive of a new revelation.

Ver. 32.

The Gentile nations of the world had failed to learn from natural reason and religion this lesson of confidence in God. Two main causes led to their failure, both of them lying very deep in the character of heathenism. For one thing, they had received no adequate revelation of God as their spiritual Father; and for want of that nearer, tenderer, and more reassuring tie, they forfeited even such assurance as they might reasonably have felt in His kindness as a faithful and provident Creator. Sinful man, it is not too much to say, cannot continue to confide even in the common providence of his Maker, so long as he knows Him only as a Maker, and not as a reconciling pardoning Father. The result, therefore, in the experience of heathens, was to banish the gods from any hearty or benevolent superintendence over the every-day affairs of private men; to put chance in the room of providence, and destiny in the seat of Deity; or, at least, to ascribe to such far-off divinities as were still supposed to take some interest in mundane affairs, a tendency to interfere with humanity in ways so capricious, partial, or mischievous, that it would have been better for them not to interfere at all. The other cause which helped to fasten down heathendom to an anxious pursuit of whatever might minister to the body, was that it had no better object set before it to pursue. Cut off from any present intercourse with the Godhead, shut in by uncertainty respecting any life to come, this life only remained to the pagan, and this life, too, on its earthly and perishing side. If the gods dwelt aloof, they had left to men at least the earth for an inheritance. If no one could say what might be after death, what could be more needful to win, or better worth enjoying, than those earthly goods which sustain and comfort this fleeting life? After all these things, therefore, did the nations of the Gentile world seek; sought them as their chief end and as the best reward of all their labour. How could the heathen spirit raise itself above an eager, sordid, and life-consuming search after things to eat or drink and raiment to put on, when there had not yet been revealed to it any Kingdom of God to be sought after?

The anxious pursuit of earthly gain, then, is simply heathenish. It consorts with a state in which man knows of no Father in heaven and no Kingdom of God on earth. But to say that, is, in the most absolute and emphatic terms, to forbid it to the Christian. Jesus addressed a company who, both as Jews, and now much more as His own pledged followers, stood on another level than the 'Gentiles.' They knew that they had a heavenly Father, a living, seeing, loving, overruling Parent, Who knew what they needed, and felt for them in their straits, and was too good to let them go without. We are no longer left to gather by the cold inferences of a creature's reason what such a Creator as we can trace by His footprints in beast and plant, may be presumed to do for us. God has spoken, not simply by nature, but across it (so to speak), and the voice that pierces the silences of creation is the voice of a Father. God has drawn the veil aside to let us see Him face to face, and the countenance we discover in Jesus Christ is the countenance of a Father. God has called us to His feet in penitence, washed us from our guilt in blood, folded us in the bliss of pardon to His heart; and the heart of which we feel the pulses beat against our own is the heart of a Father. Whoever has received a revelation like this can never more fear neglect, or starvation, or the vicissitudes of adverse fortune. Shall He Who sacrificed so much to save the souls of men, forget their bodies? He broke His Son's flesh to be a bread of life for us: will He deny us the meat that perishes? Our naked spirits, stripped of their honour through our sin, He has robed in that fair marriage-robe of linen, dazzling white, which 'is the righteousness of saints;' and need we fear for earthly raiment? What! shall a child want in his Father's house? Nay, let St. Paul expand for us in reply the splendid reasoning which lurks beneath his Master's words: 'He that spared not His own

PART I.

SECOND WARNING.

Cf. John vi. 27–58.

Rev. xix. 8.

Rom. viii. 32.

PART I.
SECOND
WARNING.

Ver. 32.

Rom. xiv. 17.

Cf. 2 Cor. v.
14, 15.

Son, but delivered Him up for us all, how shall He not with Him also freely give us all things?'

Nor is this all. Our Father has expressly released His christian family from every anxious question about earthly provision, by finding for them another and a nobler interest to care for. After food and raiment the heathen seek with absorbing eagerness, because they know no more urgent care in life than how to live. 'But seek ye first,' says Jesus, 'the kingdom of God and His righteousness.'[1] Before the soul of His disciple, this divine Restorer of the rule of God over human lives sets His own mighty task, and invites him to become His associate in the enterprise. 'The kingdom of God' *is* 'righteousness' first of all. It means the practical re-establishment of the divine authority over man's will, so that each subject returns to his allegiance, and submits to God's perfect law. It reaches this, indeed, through the manifestation of so supreme a love on God's part, love dying to reconcile and stooping to regenerate, as captures the affections of the redeemed heart. But captured affections 'constrain' to service. The pardoned rebel becomes

[1] If the reading of the Vatican MS., '*His righteousness and kingdom*,' which is preferred by Tischendorf and Lachmann, be adopted, the sense will not be materially altered. The Sinaitic reads, '*His kingdom and righteousness.*'

a loyal and law-abiding citizen under the righteous Prince. Nay, so long as his steps are among the King's foes in this revolted province, he must even be a soldier on the side of lawful authority and divine order, against anarchy, self-will, and disaffection. As yet, the Prince of Peace is a belligerent. As yet, the Prince of Righteousness labours to recover His kingdom to the Father; and no man can be deemed a true subject or honest follower who has not become inspired with an enthusiastic longing to see his Prince's mission achieved, and the Father's government re-established. Over himself, first of all, to be sure; for it is with the miniature kingdom of his own nature and the subjugation of it to the law of right, that each man has most nearly to do. He who is content to leave his private passions insubordinate, or his own life at variance with God, has no call to set himself up as the censor of other men. That is a cheap kind of loyalty to Christ which goes abroad to seek its work—preaching a kingdom of God to the world, while the inner kingdom of the heart is in the hands of lawless selfishness. Still, no one lives for himself alone. The kingdom of righteousness is struggling to get itself set up here in the midst of us—at the heart of our domestic, social, and even political arrange-

PART I.

SECOND WARNING.

Cf. 1 Cor. xv. 24–28.

Cf. below on Matt. vii. 5.

PART I.
SECOND
WARNING.

ments; and there rests on each subject of Christ a summons to do his little share on the right side, on the side of Christ's truth and God's authority and man's salvation.

Now, by his acceptance of this diviner mission, each child of God is discharged from paltry cares about meat and drink. There is, in truth, a most generous and blessed exchange of obligations betwixt Father and child. The Father's chief earthly concern, that of which, we may say with reverence, His heart of love hath most 'need,' and in which the honour of His name is most deeply engaged, is the restoration of His defied authority over His redeemed human children. With a mysterious craving for intelligent sympathy and co-operation in such an enterprise, God has charged each one who loves Him to 'seek' this 'first;' and the childlike love of each son will make ardent response. To throw himself into the thoughts of his Father, to bend his strength to the Father's work, to sacrifice personal likings, to fling aside whatever would embarrass or divert

See John iv. 34.
him, and make it his meat and drink to finish the work thus given him to do, must be the ideal of any generous child; and just as any child approaches to this ideal, will he approach the image of that perfect Child Jesus. But in

order to give himself with anything like such PART I.
single-mindedness and devotion to the kingdom SECOND
of God, a man must be set free from the distrac- WARNING.
tion of ignoble cares, and those mean anxieties
about daily bread and to-morrow's evil, which
nibble away the very pith of the soul. These,
therefore, let him cast, with a generous abandonment, on God. You have need, while you do
God's will, of food and raiment; and God knew
it when He called you to His work. It is fair,
that while He expects you to seek first His
heavenly kingdom, you should expect Him to
seek for you an earthly provision. Should the
child's heart even forget its own need to cumber
itself exclusively with the glory of its Father's
name and the coming of His realm, that blessed
Father will not be less generous in His turn, but
will take most sure care that His child shall
never want. The heart which hungers after Matt. v. 6.
righteousness shall be fed with it; the soul
athirst for God shall be 'watered' with His See 1 Cor. xii.
Spirit abundantly, and find It to be a water of $\pi\nu\epsilon\tilde{\upsilon}\mu\alpha$ $\dot{\epsilon}\pi o\tau i\sigma\theta\eta$-
life. But the bread and water which the Father $\mu\epsilon\nu$; cf. John iv. 14, vii. 38.
knows to be needful to these frail and mortal in-
struments through which alone we can meanwhile
work His will or seek His kingdom, they also
shall not fail. Rather they 'shall be added unto' Isa. xxxiii.

PART I.
SECOND WARNING.
Ver. 33, προσ-τιθήσεται.

us; thrown in along with the heavenlier things we seek, as a make-weight to turn the scale, or an overplus of bounty from the generous Father.

Cf. Phil. iv. 6.

Phil. ii. 21.

Here then, at last, we have reached Christ's effectual cure for distrustful anxiety. If, Christians as we are, with a Father in heaven to ask for bread, any poor heart among us be still fretted with fears for the morrow and the evil it may bring; may not the secret of such heathenish disquietude be found in this, that we are not flinging ourselves with sufficient self-forgetfulness into the task given us by our Father? Perhaps we are like some Christians of whom St. Paul wrote, who sought their own, not the things which are Jesus Christ's. It is when we are not pursuing as our first concern His kingdom and its righteousness, that we have room in our unfilled hearts for petty, earthly, and selfish cares. So long as we do not make God's interests our supreme care, we cannot, or we dare not, cast on God the charge of our own private interests. If we would live free of thought about to-morrow, unburdened to-day by the evil which to-morrow, when it comes, will find sufficient for itself, and would learn the secret of a heart light as a bird's in air, ought we not to practise a more entire devotion to the doing of God's righteous will and the seeking of His spiritual kingdom? Then might we say, with loyal reverence, yet with filial assurance: Lord, we are seeking that is Thine; forget not Thou to add to us what we need.

PART I.
SECOND WARNING.

For the majority of men, it is in the learning of this lesson that the chief discipline of ordinary life may be said to lie. A few are tempted by opulence, and called to withstand the seductive and fascinating gleam of gold—that mighty lord of earth, who in the end puts out the eyes and takes captive the soul of his victims. But the many must always be beset by the pressure of earthly necessities. Their way into the kingdom lies through days of toil and nights of anxiety; day and night alike taken in possession by no nobler concern than how to win for themselves and their little ones the means of subsistence. Nothing seems at first sight to stamp vanity more conspicuously on the lot of man, than to see how the earthly history of the multitude, generation after generation, may be summed up only in this: They lived that they might be able to live; they laboured that they might eat. Yet this road, worn by so many weary feet, is at least the safe one to pass through life by. The carriage way along which the rich are rolled in pride, offers

Vers. 22-24.

Matt. xix. 23, and parallels.

PART I.
SECOND
WARNING.

graver perils for the passenger than this lowly footpath. It is on the whole fortunate for the many, that their humble circumstances shield them from those all but irresistible attractions which draw the heart of the ambitious and wealthy to earth and fetter it to its treasures. It is true that squalid, hopeless penury, when long endured, is apt enough to narrow the soul, to congeal the heart, to destroy self-respect, and to put bitterness in the place at once of faith in men and faith in God. Still more often it happens that a lifelong familiarity with straits, and with that most exacting of all problems, 'What shall I eat?' drowns the soul in cares, and leaves it with as weak eyes for heavenly light, and as little room for heavenly love, as even the passion for money. Still, it seems to be in the nature of poverty to suggest God more than wealth does. When diligence is like to miss its return and foresight fails to anticipate disaster; when, after everything that human skill and toil can effect, means run short, and want like a gaunt lier in wait crouches outside the door,—then surely, if ever, is the hour to lift one's resourceless hands to Heaven in a mute appeal for that help which must come from above or not come at all. He who has no other friend, must, one would think, claim his Father's friendship. As a snow-storm will drive the wild deer from their mountains and the timid song-bird from the bough, to seek shelter and food among the dreaded dwellings of men, so may the sharp pinch of hunger send many a prodigal to his Father's table; and the cry of a hungry child is near of kin to a prayer. To be well disciplined under so stern a schoolmaster as poverty, and grow familiar with the answers which divine providence is ever sending to the appeals of want, and learn by an oft-renewed experience how blessed it is in the end to be reduced to one's last strand of dependence and hang helpless upon the bounty of the all-merciful Provider—this ought to write deep in each grateful memory an assurance of the divine faithfulness. Even those rarer straits into which most people fall at one juncture or another, when earthly resources appear to be threatened with exhaustion, and treachery or sickness or business losses have jeopardized the success of one's whole life—even such crises of anxiety bring with them an ample reward, if they teach us how to look above human aid and the ministry of second causes, and to call, in the lowliness of a child, upon Him Who feeds the raven and Who robes the lily. Viewed as an exercise-ground for such enduring

Part I.
Second Warning.

Luke xv. 14-17.

PART I.
SECOND
WARNING.

trust in God, earth assumes a nobler aspect; and the sordid lot of those who toil all their days for bread and hardly win it, becomes transfigured into glory when they are found to eat the morsel of to-day with thanks and not with tears, because they look to a Father's love for the uncertain morsel of to-morrow.

PART II.

RELATIONS TO THE WORLD AS EVIL.

OF CORRECTING THE WORLD'S EVIL.

Judge not, that ye be not judged. For with what judgment ye judge, ye shall be judged; and with what measure ye mete, it shall be measured to you [again]. And why beholdest thou the mote that is in thy brother's eye, but considerest not the beam that is in thine own eye? Or how wilt thou say to thy brother, 'Let me pull out the mote out of thine eye;' and, behold, a beam is in thine own eye? Thou hypocrite, first cast out the beam out of thine own eye; and then shalt thou see clearly to cast out the mote out of thy brother's eye. Give not that which is holy unto the dogs, neither cast ye your pearls before swine, lest they trample them under their feet, and turn again and rend you.—MATT. VII. 1-6; cf. LUKE VI. 37-42.

OF CORRECTING THE WORLD'S EVIL.

IT may be only a coincidence, but it is at least a curious one, that the word 'evil,' which suddenly appears at the close of the last paragraph, is actually as good as a cue to this new section of the sermon which opens so abruptly with the seventh chapter. It is with the moral evil which exists in the world, and with the relations sustained to it by the disciple of the kingdom, that we are now to be occupied. We have seen that the spiritual kingdom of Christ, while it holds out to our desire celestial riches and sets before us an end more to be cared for than food or raiment, does not withdraw a Christian either from the attractions of earthly wealth or from the need of earthly provision. It regulates, but does not destroy, his dealings with property. Just in the same way, the subject of Christ's new kingdom is not called upon to abandon the society of evil men, or shut his eyes to their evil acts. No sequestered retreat is

PART II.
FIRST RELATION TO EVIL.
Matt. v. 13-16.

created to which christian purity may betake itself. On the contrary, the followers of Jesus have been already told that they must shine as lights in a dark place, and act as salt upon corrupt society. It is their business to rebuke and reform those evils in the midst of which they find themselves; and that not simply by such involuntary influence as must always be exercised by a holy life (which was taught by the lamp and salt in that earlier passage), but even by direct efforts to purify the world. Here again, however, the first disciples of our King stood, as we still stand, in the utmost need of instruction; and instruction needed to take to a large extent the form of warning. No department of christian practice, indeed, is more delicate, or encompassed by graver risks, than the behaviour of christian men towards the sinful and unchristian elements which pervade society. It is so easy to condemn, without in the least reforming, or even attempting to reform, what we condemn. On the other hand, for any one to set himself up as a corrector of others in an officious or arrogant or self-righteous temper, is utterly useless; while even sincere men with the best intentions have sometimes an injudicious way of putting divine lessons before the wicked,

Of Correcting the World's Evil. 97

which is worse than useless, for it is wholly mischievous. Against all these three faulty or mistaken attitudes which Christians may assume toward evil in other people,—against simple fault-finding for fault-finding's sake, against censorious meddling, and against foolish or ill-judged ways of doing good,—our Lord proceeds in this paragraph to warn His followers.[1]

PART II.

FIRST RELATION TO EVIL.

1. What is the 'judging' so bluntly forbidden in words which, through their remarkable alliteration and close imitation of Hebrew parallelism, have made themselves almost proverbial?

'Judge not, that ye be not judged:
    For with what judgment ye judge, ye shall be judged;
    And with what measure ye measure, it shall be measured to
      you.'[2]

Vers. 1, 2.

It is superfluous to say that without a certain sort of judgment, meaning by that a discrimination betwixt good and evil, whether in actions or in actors, and a frank naming of each, where needful, by its proper name, we could never act

---

[1] The links of connection in this passage and in that which succeeds it (vers. 7-12) have been variously interpreted; and so many able expositors have even abandoned in despair the attempt to find any links of connection at all, that I venture upon the reading given in the text with the utmost diffidence.

[2] This last clause reappears in a different connection in Mark iv. 24. It was possibly proverbial before our Lord adopted it.

G

PART II.
FIRST RELATION TO EVIL.

either wisely or kindly in this world of inextricably mingled good and evil. To form, and at times to express, an opinion on the character or conduct of other men, is distinctly

John vii. 24. recognised by our Lord in another place as permissible; while the power of doing so with

1 Cor. ii. 15. truthfulness is by an apostle described as a privilege of the spiritually instructed Christian. But when Jesus adds, as His reason why we should not judge, a fear lest we may be judged in turn by the same standard, He puts into our hand a clue to the discovery of His meaning. The sort of judgment which He warns us not to pass on others is such judgment as we should not like others to pass on us. It may be a question whether the judgment we are to fear is that of our fellows or that of God Himself.

Luke vi. 37, 38. The parallel passage in St. Luke, where the idea is worked out more at large, appears to carry the former sense, when it speaks of the 'good measure, pressed down and shaken together and running over,' which 'men[1] give into the bosom' of him who gives to them. On the other hand, the impersonal form of the phrase in Matthew ('ye shall be judged'—'it shall be measured')

---

[1] We should render it 'shall *they* give' (δώσουσιν); still the use of the plural suggests that men are meant.

rather suggests a reference to the real and ultimate Judge of all. At all events, such a reference is not excluded; and we have already seen in this Sermon, that while the rule of retaliation, common as it actually is among men, can never be a safe rule for us, it is nevertheless God's everlasting axiom of justice and the foundation of all right jurisprudence. Both with a view, therefore, to the criticisms which our neighbours may pass, with or without reason, upon our conduct, and with regard to the final award of Heaven, our Lord bids us judge others only as we would have others to judge us.

_{PART II.}
_{FIRST RELATION TO EVIL.}
_{Matt. v. 38.}

What kinds of judgment this will exclude we can be at no loss to discover. No one likes, for example, to have the worst possible construction put upon his conduct. There are some people who, like carrion-birds, have the keenest scent for garbage, and will fly far to seek it; who always suspect base reasons for whatever looks generous, and exult in exposing them to view: but we are not apt to conclude that such men's own motives are the purest or their own life the sweetest in the world. We pay them back in their own coin. Neither does any one like to be at once condemned on external or *primâ facie* evidence. We all know our own motives better than our critics do; and we know how, when our actions look most suspicious, there are concealed facts which, if known, would put a better colour on the case. Therefore let none of us be so unfair, not to say ungracious, as to condemn his neighbour on mere surface appearances or on idle suspicion; nay, nor prematurely to pronounce upon his neighbour's motives at all; since, so long as the hidden things of the heart are hidden, we cannot without risk of error presume to sit in judgment on the real moral condition of any man. It is the Lord Who at His coming will both 'bring to light the hidden things of darkness, and will make manifest the counsels of the hearts.' Even as regards plain and patent faults of the outer life, there are people so ready at fault-finding, so scant in praise, so untender in trumpeting to the world their neighbour's failing, and so provokingly condescending when they mention it to himself, that everybody shrinks from them as by instinct. Faults are the sores of character; and just as one guards a wound, and resents the needless or ungentle touch of merely curious bystanders, so do we with the fault-finder. Therefore let us not be forward to point the finger at flaws in others which, however patent, we should not care to have pointed out in ourselves. Nay, this same test is delicate enough to condemn even such private criticism upon a brother as I may forbear to utter and lock up in my own breast. How should I feel if I only knew that my fair-spoken companion was mentally making ungracious comments on me, or passing upon my character an unuttered condemnation? Would not the bare suspicion of such secret censoriousness freeze up affection, and rear betwixt us an ice-wall of distrust? We have to live with one another; and the kindly thoughts of others about ourselves is as the breath of life to us. The more sensitive any one is to praise or blame,—the more he would resent gratuitous fault-finding as an impertinence, or be pained by ungenerous imputations as a wrong,—so much the slower ought he to be to expose the weak points of other men, or to reflect upon their motives. Nay, more: if we would escape not only the harsh and unfair condemnation of men, but far more the rigorous and unmitigated justice of Heaven, it behoves us to turn our judgment into charity. Instead of filling up a brimming measure with accusations and insinuations and sneers and the cold censure of the self-righteous, let us rather give liberally of our most kindly and pardoning charity. Fill up the measure with that love

PART II.

FIRST RELATION TO EVIL.

Cf. Prov. x. 12; c. 1 Pet. iv. 8.

which hopes for the best, finds excuses for the bad, and would gladly cover over the worst; fill it up, and press it down, and shake it well together, and brim it to the lip till it overflows, for it will return. Such measure will the thankful hearts of men pour back into your bosom. Human nature is not so bad but it will answer yet to kindness; men press the hand that presses theirs. While surely a day is coming when, before the face of a righteous Judge, the best of us will have need of all the mercy that he has shown to others.

It is, in truth, the consciousness of our own faults which alone can make us tender to the faults of others. Therefore the strongly metaphorical proverb by which our Lord proceeds to teach that self-knowledge is the mother of charity, though it is introduced mainly for another end, does really cast back important light on His opening words against 'judging.' That the man with the biggest beam in his own eye is apt to be the severest censor of his brother's mote, is true to human experience. For this very reason, uncharitable judgment is precisely that fault from which a Christian ought to be exceptionally free. Does not a profound and heart-burdening consciousness of one's own sin lie at the base of christian character? Is it not through the humiliation of a contrite self-condemnation that every soul must enter into the kingdom of God? Has not Jesus opened this discourse by blessing the poor, the mournful, and the meek? Yet, while christian repentance, where it is genuine, must always save a man from sitting in judgment upon his brother, the self-righteousness of human nature, reappearing in Christianity as it appeared in Judaism, has constantly led to the very opposite result. There is no one so prone to pass severe and unnecessary censure, as he who imagines that he has entered the kingdom of heaven by some other door, without having passed through this strait gate of penitence. To take one's self for a Christian, and yet be ignorant of the extent of one's own guilt and evil-heartedness, is to be exactly in that state of blind conceit which qualifies a man for the *rôle* of a heartless and reckless and utterly unrighteous judge. We see it every day: men whose religion consists in little else than indiscriminate abuse of the rest of the world, who never try to understand the temptations of the fallen, nor ever put out a hand to help them, but are content from some serene summit of implied superiority to survey with a wondering pity the miserable condition of common sinners, to measure by their own standard the criminality of whole classes and races of their fellow-men and utter over them glib sentences of condemnation, without one touch of that divine compassion which makes its brother's case its own and sorrows where it is forced to blame. It is true that all Christians are not to be reckoned in this unlovely class whom the world reckons in it. The world can misjudge as well as the Christian. Indeed, how could it be expected that the world, whose sins are by the Church rebuked, should always do justice to the motives of its rebuker? On the other hand, it is idle to deny that nothing else has ever done so much as religionists of this type have done to defame religion and caricature the spirit of Christianity.

2. The case is not mended when a censorious Christian, not content with barren censorship, volunteers to correct the faults which he condemns. To stand aloof, an idle spectator of the evil that is in the world, remarking and criticising each mote in our neighbour's eye in that ungracious temper which comes from ignorance of the beam in one's own—this judicial attitude toward the wicked world is not the christian attitude. A servant of Christ should try to make

the bad better. Suppose, then, that, passing from the office of a judge to the office of a reformer, the Christian carries with him the same ignorance of himself which made him an unfair judge, will it not now make him also a bungling reformer? If it was out of place to set up as the censurer of your brother's mote when your own faults were to his as a plank to a splinter, it is surely still more out of place to set yourself up for his corrector. The comparison sounds extravagant; since, though minute fragments from a twig may get into the eye and need to be taken out, to speak of a great beam of timber[1] in the same connection is absurd. The extravagance of the phrase, however, did not hinder its being a usual and accepted one in oriental speech; and as such our Lord borrowed it to point His moral. What that moral is, is plain enough. In the first place, it is in a preposterous degree unbecoming to be so quick to see, much more to propose to mend, small faults in another when one's own are so very great. It is, as we say, like 'Satan reproving sin.' Besides, it is not only a grotesque betrayal of self-ignorance, but a presumptuous over-esti-

PART II.
FIRST RELATION TO EVIL.

Ver. 4.

---

[1] δοκός means properly such a 'beam' as is fit to be employed for the joist or rafter of a building. κάρφος, again, denotes a minute splinter, as of brushwood.

mate of one's own ability. To mend a brother's fault, one has need of a most clear and undistorted spiritual vision, an eye of the soul quite single and limpid. No task asks cleaner motives, or truer insight, or more of that perfect fairness which can only spring from love, than this task of a reformer of manners. I can scarcely doubt that, by the selection of this metaphor, our Lord meant to hint that the self-ignorance which sets itself to correct others before it has corrected itself, or even detected its own need of correction, is just the moral condition which of all others disqualifies a man for such an enterprise. The speck you think you have discerned in your brother may be nothing else than the projection of a false image from your own distempered character. 'How canst thou say to thy brother, "Brother, let me put out the mote that is in thine eye," when thou thyself beholdest not the beam that is in thine own eye?' Or, as our Lord developes His thought in words omitted from St. Matthew's report: 'Can the blind lead the blind? Shall they not both fall into the ditch? The disciple is not above his master.'

But there is more to be said than this. The interference of such blind guides and ignorant teachers is worse than a blunder. It is an hypocrisy. You profess to be so deeply concerned for the faults of your neighbour, that you would fain do him a service by ridding him of them: you are ardent in the interest of his reformation, a self-constituted preacher of righteousness. That looks well. But if it were really concern for the correction of evil and the cure of souls which inspired this officious zeal of yours, would it not show itself first of all in the reformation of yourself? A very little honest desire to have God's kingdom come and His will done would suffice to reveal to yourself how much more shameful and painful your own moral disorders are than any you propose to remedy; and in the hard task of casting out your own huge sins of heart, you would find work enough to keep your hands full. The *tu quoque* rejoinder, 'Physician, heal thyself,' is in its place here. 'First cast out the beam.' This very officiousness in well-doing, this arrogant setting up as a corrector of morals, this immodest and loveless meddling with your neighbours—what is it but a sign how pride has made you stone-blind, and a proof that it is not the sympathy of a penitent which inspires you, but the conceit of a fault-finder?

What then? Is there to be no mending of the evil attempted? Must christian men for-

PART II.
FIRST RELATION TO EVIL.

bear such a delicate and perilous office altogether? Not so. No man dare do that: least of all the man who calls himself a follower of Jesus Christ. Only let self-correction have the first place: first in time, inasmuch as till the biggest of all beams have been cast out—the beam of ignorant self-conceit, and that uncharitableness which goes along with it—I can have neither clearness of eye nor skill and softness of touch to do my brother any real good; but first always in place, since, however I may busy myself with the reformation of other men, I must to the very end be still more busy with my own. If Christians were more self-distrustful, more penetrated with a contrite longing after personal holiness, and more rigorous to mark and to amend their private failings, how much less heart would they have to become volunteer fault-finders or fault-menders, where they have no business; but also, how much more able to see truly, and judge candidly, and cast out with lowly tenderness and patience, every speck in the character of those with whose character it concerns them as their brothers to meddle! We should then have a deal more of quiet, effective, and kindly casting out of motes; but far fewer of such offers as this, spoken in blunt offensive fashion, 'Let me pull it out!'

3. There is still a third way in which good men may err in their efforts to do good. Only this third error differs from the other two so far as to form almost an antithesis to them. Beneath both the mistakes already indicated, that of idle criticism upon faults, and that of self-righteous attempts to correct them, there lies an excessive proneness to see evil in others, and to condemn it. It is possible, however, to fail on the opposite extreme. One may see in other men too little evil. There are in this world a number of unhappy persons to whose insolent or fleshly minds the most sacred things have no sacredness, and the most precious things no preciousness; and there are good souls who carry their charity so far that they ignore the real character of such profane or sensual persons, and refuse to treat them as if they were as evil as they are. Instead of being too ready to call evil, evil, and to deal with it accordingly, these weak but well-meaning Christians act as if all men must be good enough at least to esteem and reverence what is good. They blunder with the best intentions: not through want of kindliness, but through defect of wisdom; not from judging too severely, but from refusing to judge at all. The robust good sense which informed our perfect Master

PART II.

FIRST RELATION TO EVIL.

Ver. 6.

saw that it was necessary to recognise facts. Let the fact be frankly faced, that there are men who, in their relations to the kingdom of God and its sacred blessings, are like the homeless, shameless dogs of an eastern city, or the foul and fierce swine which it was forbidden to a Jew so much as to herd. In their eyes the holiest things are common. The sacred flesh of our christian table they will eat without 'discerning the Lord's body.' To their earthly taste, the costliest treasure of the spiritual life, though it were the 'Pearl of great price,' is valueless compared to the swinish delights of appetite. It is no breach of charity to recognise the incapacity of such men for heavenly truth. It is a breach alike of prudence and of reverence not to recognise it. You gain nothing by treating a dog as if it were not a dog; and you gain nothing by throwing away sacred privileges on men who have shown that they will only abuse them. The law of charity, it is true, requires a generous treatment even of the worst; but charity itself must acknowledge that what would be suitable and kindly behaviour to one man, to another will be simply mischievous. Give to swine what swine can appreciate—beans, not pearls; else the disappointed brute, when it has trampled your offering in the mire, may turn

Of Correcting the World's Evil. 111

with the rage of a boar 'and rend you.' If we stultify our attempts to reform the vicious and brutal by plans which may look charitable, but are simply childish, winking at the darker facts of human character, we have ourselves to thank for it, should the indiscreet missionary find his intentions misunderstood and his pains thrown away. Nor is it only the truth and its preacher that suffer; the sinner himself is made worse. To bring bad men, by ill-judged methods, and at ill-chosen times, into contact with the holy lessons of our christian faith, so that the holy is turned into contempt and the precious rejected with insolent profanity, is really to misguide our fallen brethren into a deeper guilt, and to translate their profligacy into sacrilege. It is true that the gospel is to be preached to all men, and that when fitly preached it is the power of God to the salvation of all; but 'a wise man's heart discerneth both time and judgment.' To select the fit occasion and discover the wise method; to adapt truth to the evil state of the hearer, and win for it a willing ear; to be cautious without being timid, and faithful but not indiscreet: this asks for a certain nice tact or indefinable instinct which is given to few, a wisdom into which there enter many elements,

PART II.
FIRST RELATION TO EVIL.

Rom. i. 16.
Eccles. viii. 5.

PART II.
FIRST
RELATION TO
EVIL.

but of which one element surely is a spiritual gift from the Father of lights.

Looking back now over these directions, to sum up their result, we gather, although it is from negatives, a pretty full conception of how Christians ought to act towards the world's sin. To recognise the evil that is in other men is not forbidden; but we are forbidden to sit in judgment on it, as if we were simply our brother's critics. The critical attitude in one sinful man towards the sin of others shows that he forgets his own. His judgment will probably be unfair; it cannot fail to be unmerciful. The evil, therefore, which we find ourselves unable to mend, we are not called upon to judge. But even our efforts to mend evil must be limited, on the one side, by such a modest and lowly charity as springs from self-discipline, and on the other by a wise and reverential caution. If we set ourselves to make other men better without having first bettered ourselves, we fall into hypocritical meddling; if without the prudence which grows from knowledge of evil and reverence for truth, we become intemperate zealots. For the failings of the weak we need the tenderness of sympathy; for the vices of the profane, the tenderness of prudence. Though the one error, that of ungenerous and meddlesome fault-finding, is very much more common than the second, being indeed (as some one says) 'the sorest plague in social life;' it is worth remarking that both faults are specially frequent in young or inexperienced disciples. The new convert, having just discovered the evil of sin in himself, is specially sensitive to remark it in others, and at once applies to it his new and more exacting standard of judgment. With a promptitude untempered by disappointment, he is forward to censure older brethren, under the generous persuasion that faults need only to be known in order to be corrected. With equal eagerness he expects that the blessed gospel truths which wear for him their first sanctity undimmed, must at once command the homage of the worst of men. Under all this there is much rawness of judgment and ignorance of himself. By and by, when the 'dim perilous' fight with sin in his own heart has taught the Christian, at the cost of falls and tears, how hard it is to cast out one 'beam,' he will grow more merciful to his brother, and speak less harshly of his errors. Experience, too, in attempting the recovery of the lawless and sensual, is sure to beget a salutary caution, and a

PART II.

FIRST RELATION TO EVIL.

more delicate recognition of the relations which the various parts of sacred truth bear to the various characters of men. Yet to the last the ripest Christian and the best practised will find it a task of extreme difficulty to handle holy themes with awe while aiming at the conscience of the profane, and will discover increasing cause to wonder at the insensibility, as well as at the depravity, of human nature.

OF ESCAPING THE WORLD'S EVIL.

Ask, and it shall be given you; seek, and ye shall find; knock, and it shall be opened unto you: for every one that asketh, receiveth; and he that seeketh, findeth; and to him that knocketh, it shall be opened. Or what man is there of you, whom, if his son ask bread, will he give him a stone? Or if he ask a fish, will he give him a serpent? If ye then, being evil, know how to give good gifts unto your children, how much more shall your Father Which is in heaven give good things to them that ask Him? Therefore all things whatsoever ye would that men should do to you, do ye even so to them: for this is the Law and the Prophets. Enter ye in at the strait gate: for wide is the gate, and broad is the way, that leadeth to destruction, and many there be which go in thereat: because strait is the gate, and narrow is the way, which leadeth unto life, and few there be that find it.—MATT. VII. 7–14.

Cf. LUKE XI. 9–13, VI. 31, XIII. 23, 24.

OF ESCAPING THE WORLD'S EVIL.

IT is at this passage of our Lord's discourse that it becomes most difficult to trace with confidence the thread of connection; so difficult, that some expositors have despaired of finding any thread of connection at all.[1] If the attempt I am about to make have any success, its success will best appear by its preserving unbroken through these seemingly disjointed sentences the clue of thought which we have hitherto been following.

PART II.

SECOND RELATION TO EVIL.

In the first six verses of this chapter, we have found our Teacher defining the attitude which His disciple ought to hold who desires to correct evil in other men. The general result of that definition has been decidedly discouraging. It is a vastly easier matter to censure evil than to correct it. The first condition of correcting the evil of others is to have corrected it in one's self. Even where the motives are quite sincere, it is the most delicate of all offices. On the one side lies a style of fault-finding which sins through defect

Vers. 1-6.

[1] As Meyer, for example.

PART II.
SECOND RELATION TO EVIL.

of charity, and on the other such an ignoring of faults as works mischief through defect of wisdom. Our Lord's directions how to influence the world for its good have resolved themselves into nothing else but a string of warnings against mistakes.

Under these circumstances, one sees that the existence of evil in the world around him becomes for every christian disciple an influential —perhaps the most influential—factor in his own spiritual self-discipline. It is not simply the Christian who is to act upon the evil world: the evil world will react powerfully upon the Christian. He cannot escape it, either by fleeing from its presence or by shutting his eyes to its offensiveness. He must neither affect to treat its wickedness as if it were not the thing it is, nor presume to look down on those who do it from some superior judgment-seat, as though he had no share in it. The evil which is in his brother is in himself as well; and with that evil, first in himself and then in his brother, he is forced to deal, holding it for what it is, and seeking as best he can to cast it out. Now, if there is anything about the position of a disciple in this life fitted to act upon him as a discipline, driving him back upon a superhuman source of

Of Escaping the World's Evil. 119

strength, educating him in practical self-control, and steeling him to an exceptional earnestness of temper, it is this incessant contact with the mighty mass of secular evil and the inevitable necessity of contending with it. It is not too much to say that Christ leaves His few and scattered servants alone in the world with this express design, that it should become an exercise ground for training them, as nowhere else could they be so well trained, in those arduous virtues which are distinctively christian—the humility of dependence on God, the nobler retaliation which gives good for evil, and the intense spiritual resolution which dares to be singular for the sake of God.

PART II.
SECOND RELATION TO EVIL.

Cf. John xvii. 15-19.

Here, then, have we not a key to the three exhortations which immediately follow the three warnings of last paragraph? (1.) It is not in others only, but in yourself, that the evil dwells against which you are bound to war; and the self-discipline which casts out your own faults is the sole condition of your being fit to correct a brother with the humility of charity and the discretion that comes by experience. The slightest effort to do good is enough to teach a man how helpless he is in such self-discipline. Therefore you must fall back upon a help which

Vers. 7-14.

Marginalia: PART II. SECOND RELATION TO EVIL. Vers. 7-11. Cf. Luke xi. 13. Ver. 12. Rom. xii. 21. Vers. 13, 14.

is not within you, but above. Prayer, which is the voice of dependence urged by need, is the secret of spiritual improvement. Instead of judging, therefore, pray. Ask with importunity, and an urgency which takes no denial, for the cleansing of your own inward eye, for purity and lowliness, and wisdom: ask the Father's good gift of His Holy Spirit for yourself first, and then for those whose faults you seek to mend. (2.) Moreover, the continual presence of evil men is a continual provocation to the evil in your own heart. It brings with it a temptation to retaliate in kind, to measure back to others in their own vessel. Be on your guard, therefore, and remember that it is not men's treatment of you, but what your own self-love would desire their treatment to be, which gives law to you. 'Be not overcome of evil, but overcome evil with good.' (3.) After all, it is hard to be so unlike your fellow-men. This evil world is so vast, so mighty, so omnipresent, so overwhelming in its rush after godless delights, that it will need a very resolute will and a rigorous denial of self to withstand the sympathy of numbers, and press from the broad, easy, crowded road of sin into that narrow path of holy obedience which God has fenced so straitly on either hand.

Whether or not this be the hidden connection of thought betwixt these two sections, it may be said that we have before us, in brief pithy words of exhortation, three leading rules for the conduct of christian life as affected by the evil world. Jesus has summed up the posture which becomes His follower, according to a well-known scheme which distinguishes our duty as threefold: bearing reference to God, to our neighbour, and to ourselves. As St. Paul did after His example, so he bids us, if we would 'deny' the 'ungodliness and worldly lusts' in the midst of which our path must lie, live godly, righteous, and sober lives: godly, in the dependence of faith on the gifts of the Father; righteous, after a 'golden rule' of generous neighbourliness; and sober, with a strict avoidance of the lawless latitude which other men permit themselves. But, through all these words of exhortation, I catch an undertone of earnestness, intense enough to be called severe, as of One Who felt that to lead such a life in such a world was no child's play for the strongest, but asked of him who should succeed in it, the strain of a mighty purpose, forged perchance in some heat of passion, but beaten into tenacity through the exigencies and endurance of a lifelong labour.

PART II.

SECOND RELATION TO EVIL.

Tit. ii. 12.

PART II.
SECOND
RELATION TO
EVIL.
Vers. 7, 8.

I. Such earnest urgency certainly breathes through His call to prayer. The emphatic reduplication of the injunction marks what stress the Speaker laid upon it. So does the rising scale of intensity in the words employed: ask—seek—knock. To 'seek' is a more industrious and solicitous and animated kind of asking. We ask for what we want; we seek for that which we have lost: and this sense of loss sharpens at once our need and our desire. Again: to 'knock' is a description of seeking at once most helpless and most importunate; since he who seeks admission at his friend's door has nothing else to do but go on knocking till he be answered. The asker will study how best to state his plea when once he gains a hearing, but may never care to seek another opportunity. The seeker will make, or watch for, opportunities of access to the patron whose favourable ear he hopes to gain, but, often baffled, may grow weary in his efforts. The knocker must simply trust to the force of patience and of repetition, sure that if he knock loud enough he shall be heard, and, if he continue to knock long enough, he must be attended to. It would be impossible to teach with greater emphasis the idea that prayer is a laborious and enduring exercise of the human spirit, to which

Of Escaping the World's Evil. 123

we need to be moved by a vivid, unresting, neverending experience of our own need, and in which we ought to be sustained by a fixed certainty that God will hear us in the end.

The subject of prayer fills a large place in the recorded teaching of our blessed Lord; and this duty of unwearied perseverance in asking what has been promised, but is not at once conceded, stands out as the most characteristic of His lessons. On at least two distinct and later occasions, reported by St. Luke, Jesus repeated the exhortation to continue praying until we receive. On each occasion He enforced it by an analogy, drawn once from the private and once from the public relations of men. The householder who is induced to rise from bed at an inconvenient hour of night, simply to be rid of the disturbance caused by his neighbour's persistent knocking, and the judge who takes up the cause of a poor widow only when her 'continual coming' has worried him into reluctant compliance, are parallels which stand of course in flagrant contrast to God's treatment of our petitions, so far as the motives go which ultimately lead to a favourable hearing; but they agree at least in this point, that it is perseverance in asking which wins the day. Nay, this con-

Luke xi. 5-8.

Luke xviii. 1-8.

PART II.
SECOND RELATION TO EVIL.

trast, which at first sight shocks us, betwixt the disinclination of a lazy neighbour to oblige, or of a corrupt magistrate to do justice where he is not bribed to do it, and the infinite readiness of our heavenly Father's love, is actually fitted, or perhaps designed, to strengthen the argument for importunity. For if, even on the low ground of selfishness, perseverance prevails over the unwilling, how much more certain is it to prevail

Isa. lxv. 24.

with Him Whose generosity needs no spur, but waits only for a call to bless!

The argument *à fortiori*, which in these later parables is pushed to such an extreme as almost to run some risk of misconception, appears also in the text; but here it appears under a different connection, and in a form which effectually shuts out misconception. Instead of building on those infirmities of human nature, which allow of its being pestered into compliance even when better

Vers. 9–11.

motives fail, our Lord builds here on that which is the very best thing left in our ruined human nature—the divine instinct of parenthood. The tie of parent to child, with the sweet confiding and obedient dependence which marks it on the one side, and the generous capacity for self-devotion which is its glory on the other, is our chief earthly emblem for that most sacred and tender of all conceivable bonds, the bond which links the Eternal Father above to the soul of His redeemed human creature. On this analogy our Lord's whole teaching, like His whole life, hung suspended; and throughout this Sermon it has run in and out like a thread of silver, uniting while it lights up the whole. But the appeal to our emblematic human fatherhood, which underlies so many passages, and glances forth here and there in momentary allusions, comes at this point quite plainly to the surface. It is when we are petitioners for the gifts of God that we take most unmistakeably the attitudes of children, and may most confidently expect Him to meet us with the welcome of a parent. Sometimes men ask from men, but commonly with more or less of that reluctance which springs from the pride of equality : children ask always from their parents, and feel no shame. Sometimes men give to men, but often from baser motives than generosity, or in hope to receive as much, or with the secret pride of having laid an equal under obligation : parents give always to their children, and, through the purity of their love, feel no pride. In no other relation which we know is so much asked or given; asked with such frank confidence, or given with such ungrudging readiness. It is, in

PART II.

SECOND RELATION TO EVIL.

Cf. v. 9, 16, 45, vi. 1, 9, 26, 32.

> PART II.
> SECOND RELATION TO EVIL.

fact, the badge of childhood and its privilege—to ask and get; the joy of parents and their honour—to be asked and give. Can we be the children of God, and not use the privilege of our peculiar position to ask Him for the things we need? Or shall we have leave to use our privilege of asking, and yet find that He denies Himself on His part the joy of giving?

> Heb. viii. 5.

This 'example and shadow of heavenly things' which is offered to our study in every well-ordered family on earth is more than an analogy, it is an argument; and it might conceivably have been employed by our Lord to enforce His urgent call in the previous sentence to importunity in prayer. For it surely belongs to the fatherliness of God that He will not leave His child to cry on for ever without an answer. Our Lord's distinct assurance, therefore, given in words

> Vers. 7, 8.

which recapitulate His first promise in order to individualize it, that 'every one' who asks and seeks and knocks shall in the end be listened to, might very well have been made to rest on the fact that He to Whom we pray is no slothful neighbour or unrighteous judge, but our own Father. Only the cry of a child hardly needs to be repeated in order to reach its parent's heart. On the contrary, the infirmity of parenthood leans rather to indulgence than to refusal. So far from leaving the child to wail on unheeded in its hunger or pain, the weak heart of earthly fathers is only too easily moved by the impatient or foolish clamour of childhood to grant requests which are no boons, and give what were better withheld. Accordingly, the parable is made to yield a different lesson. It is not the certainty that parents will attend at last to the plaintive and repeated cry of little ones which is made to testify of God; for so much may well be taken for granted. It is rather the wisdom of parents in knowing what to give and what to withhold, on which our thoughts are now fastened. Ready enough—and sometimes too ready—to give, the father is still wise enough also to give on the whole with discrimination. 'Ye know how to give good gifts:' that is the point of the lesson. The round white stone may have some slight resemblance to a cake of bread; and snakes as well as fishes have cold and glistening scales.[1] But love is too careful to be deceived, and too kind to deceive. It will neither give at haphazard and by mistake what may prove useless or hurtful,

[1] On the occasion in Luke (xi. 12) a third example is added, that of the egg and scorpion. Here the idea of a superficial deceptive resemblance must apparently be abandoned. See Thomson, *Land and Book* (p. 246, London ed.).

nor will it deliberately mock the hunger of its child by offering apparent blessings for real ones. So far from that, it will not even humour the mistaken longings of the child himself. For if the foolish infant, misled by appearances, should cry for a stone instead of bread, or take the glittering adder for a wholesome fish, even human parental love is wise enough to deny the prayer that asks amiss, and, reading behind such childish words the child's true need, will refuse the evil to bestow the good. Men are at their best bad (according to the witness of this Man, Who, with an involuntary consciousness of His own moral isolation, holds Himself strangely aloof while He addresses all other men as 'ye who are evil'); and from the fatherliness of even the best of bad men to the fatherliness of Him Who alone is 'good' is a long inference. But the worst of fathers, as well as the best, are fathers still. We credit even the most ignorant or negligent of parents with sufficient love, not merely to hearken when his child calls, but also to interpret inarticulate cries, to anticipate unspoken wants, to correct mistaken requests, to refuse what is asked in folly, and generally to know how to give gifts that are truly 'good.' Even in the wreck of our race, where humanity, starved and savage, has become most thoroughly 'evil,' we still look to see so much of this parental love and wisdom shining in the darkest place; or, if we fail to find it, our sense is shocked as by something monstrous in nature. Can we measure, then, the force of our Lord's 'How much more!' or estimate the contrast which so glorious an *à fortiori* implies betwixt this feeble spark of fatherhood which He has been at pains to spare, in order that, amid the evil earth, it might still glimmer forth some pale witness to Himself, and that fulness of unexhausted paternity, of infinite tenderness led by unsearchable wisdom, which dwells within the bosom of the Heavenly Father?

Here, in these simple, homely, human words of Jesus, we have surely all the philosophy of prayer which christian hearts require. They are the words of One Whose own history gave the example which elucidates the precept. It was a Son's life which He brought down to earth from the unseen heaven: and the voice of His human sonship to God was prayer. Prayers like His are impossible to one who is not, like Him, a child of God; to any one who is, they are simply unavoidable. Whatever He felt Himself in want of, He asked; for the simple reason that His life as a Son had its root in the life of the

PART II.

SECOND RELATION TO EVIL.

Cf. Isa. xlix. 15.

Ver. 11.

I

Father, was fed from the spiritual and temporal supplies of the Father, and looked up to that Parent to do a parent's service. When He asked once and was not answered, He asked again, and yet again; just because He was sure the Father, being a father, must hear. A good son can afford to wait a good father's time. Whatever desire pressed upon His heart, He uttered in a petition, even though through a child's infirmity the cry pressed out by anguish might be a mistaken one, asking what was less good than the best; for He could trust His Father with wisdom enough to discern, and love enough to bestow, only the best gifts. Therefore, to all such requests as expressed the longing of mere earthly infirmity—infirmity without sin—He added the modest and dutiful 'nevertheless' of a little child. It is not given to children always to know stones from bread, and no father would prohibit or chide the frank utterance of whatever his child desires; but it is given to true children to know that they are but children, and to ask with deferential 'fear,' reckoning their petitions to be only petitions, not demands. Such children, like Jesus, will be heard in that they fear; and will get, if not what they ask, yet certainly what they want. For all genuine intercourse betwixt child and parent must have two sides: while it is on the child's side the freest and most unlimited expression of such things as a child's heart can long for, or a child's judgment discern to be good, it is on the parent's side also the freest and most voluntary determination to give only what a riper judgment knows to be best, and all that a larger heart yearns to bestow.

The truth is, this filial spirit in prayer is impossible unless the petitioner have the most ample leave to say to his Father everything, wise or foolish, which he desires to say; to ask for everything, good or not so good, which he desires to have. The idea of arbitrary limitation from without contradicts the filial relation. At the same time, the intelligence or modesty of the child himself, his acquaintance with his Father's purposes, and his own judgment of what is either possible or desirable, will always determine the limitations which he himself will impose upon his own petitions. Requests which are possible to one of the family may thus be impossible to another, or needless to a third. He who has penetrated furthest into the mind of the Father, will of course ask most nearly what the Father is prepared to grant. But though such a wise son will offer his petition with less hesitation than another, or with

PART II.
SECOND
RELATION TO
EVIL.

greater confidence that he will get the very thing he asks for, yet he need not be one whit more confident than the most ignorant or blundering of his brothers, that whatever is best for him will be the answer of the Father. Rather, a child may trust the Parent's wisdom most, precisely where it can trust its own the least; and be exercising the noblest and most heroic faith, faith which honours and pleases the Father best, when it dares ask for nothing, but has this for its only cry, mixed with tears and sobs: 'Not what I will, but what Thou wilt.'

Mark xiv. 36.

The 'good things' which Jesus declares His Father ready to give 'to them that ask Him' are not to be narrowed down to any single department of a Christian's life. They must be taken to cover an area as wide and varied as the wants which God's children have to tell to their Father. In that passage of St. Luke's Gospel, however, where Jesus repeats these sentences almost *verbatim* upon a subsequent occasion, He substitutes for these 'good things' the one comprehensive and magnificent gift of 'the Holy Spirit.' Within the new kingdom of our Father, this personal coming of the Third Person as the gift promised by the Father and conferred through the Son, covers all spiritual 'good things,' so as fully to

Luke xi. 13.

Acts i. 4, ii. 33.

Of Escaping the World's Evil. 133

satisfy every spiritual desire of the filial heart: since what we earthly sons of God are now taught to desire is summed up in this one thing, to be made like Him Who is the type of sonship and perfect image of our Father; and this desire must find its fulfilment, if the same Spirit Who inspired the sonship of Jesus, and wrought in Him the image of God, be given to dwell also in us, and work within us the same character. While therefore temporal blessings are not excluded, but included, the immediate design and emphasis of the passage is to throw us back upon God as petitioners for such spiritual gifts as belong to character. To this also the connection leads. This injunction to pray does not follow at once upon the warning against amassing secular wealth, and the dissuasives from secular care. It follows those verses in which the Lord has pointed out the duties of a disciple to the sin that is in the world. The 'good things,' therefore, which immediately and in the first instance He bids us ask for, are such as these: spiritual skill to discern the evil and the good; reverence enough not to expose sacred things to contempt; a purged and clear eye to correct men's sins with; a large measure of charity; the humility of self-knowledge, and the tenderness which grows from self-amend-

PART II.
SECOND
RELATION TO
EVIL.

Rom. viii. 29.

Ibid. 9-15.

Ch. vi. 19-34.

Ch. vii. 1-6.

PART II.
SECOND
RELATION TO
EVIL.

vi. 25 ff.
vi. 19 ff.
vi. 1 ff.
v. 17-48.

ment. It may well be that Jesus means to cast His eye back over a still larger tract of His foregoing discourse, and bids us beg God for such 'good things' as a trustful, contented temper, a heart set on heavenly treasures, a sincere regard to God in secret, and that divine righteousness which keeps the law in its spirit, and is all compact of love itself. The whole sum, indeed, of that perfection to which our King has been calling His followers throughout the legislative sections of this inaugural Sermon is to be asked as a gift from our Father in heaven; for if we could not ask it and receive it as a gift wrought in us for Jesus' sake by His Holy Spirit, then Jesus would be no King of Salvation, but only a legislator more exacting than Moses, and His gospel no tidings of gladness, but a yoke more intolerable than the law. Commonly, however, it is the impact of his new-born zeal against the rough edge of sin which first teaches the christian convert his need of a divine strength. All things seem possible to the enthusiasm of a young disciple, till he tries. But whenever a christian man begins to take up in earnest the task of reforming the evil around him, and of doing it in the right way, he is presently forced to his knees. He who would touch other men's sins with gentle,

Of Escaping the World's Evil. 135

wise, or lowly love, must first look well to his personal sinfulness; and the honest effort to have his own faults cast out and his heart made pure, will open up to him the breadth of Christ's gospel law of holiness, and teach him how it embraces every detail of life, penetrates our secret motives, and summons us to a purity, truthfulness, and charity which are to be perfect with the perfections of God. Actual contact with evil after Christ's own manner, actual efforts to be good enough to do any good in an evil earth, will always drive home such a discouraging conviction of helplessness; and it is when His honest follower is in this baffled, resourceless mood, facing sin as a fact which he can neither expel from his own nor from other men's lives, that Jesus takes him as it were by the hand, and with eyes devoutly lifted to the Father, says to him, 'Let us pray.'

I suppose the frequency or strength of a Christian's impulse to cry for spiritual help may thus be taken as a safe gauge of the thoroughness with which he has entered on the Lord's battle against sin. Nor will any experienced combatant in this moral war be at a loss to recognise the reason why Christ's words take at this point a certain terse sharpness as of a battle-cry, or why He is fain to

PART II.

SECOND RELATION TO EVIL.

Cf. v. 48.

<small>PART II.
SECOND
RELATION TO
EVIL.</small>

reiterate with growing urgency His call to prayer, or why He asseverates His assurance some six times over that the help will surely come. For this contest with sin, inside and outside of christian life, is a sore, tedious, baffling, wearing-out sort of contest, in which one is so often beaten that nothing save the sharpest need could prevail upon one not to give over praying in despair. But to give over praying means giving over fighting; and to give over fighting means giving over <small>Eccles. viii. 8.</small> Christ. 'There is no discharge in this war,' any more than in our war with death. The longer it goes on, the hotter it waxes. Asking for the Spirit of Help must grow into an anxious seeking for Him; and seeking without finding may give place to a persistent day-after-day knocking with the same knock at Heaven's gate for the aid which delays to come. And still our need of our Father's gifts goads us to beg again for them; and still the faint heart rouses itself once more at the urgent iteration of its King: 'Every one that asketh, receiveth; and he that seeketh, findeth; and to him that knocketh, it shall be opened.'

At last, oh at last, when this lifelong discipline of need and longing and trust and patience <small>Cf. Jas. i. 2-5.</small> and importunity has done its slow but perfect work, and tempered the disciple into the temper desired of God, then the answer, which has been coming unperceived and in disguised shapes all along, bursts in one day of joy upon the petitioner. The full gift of the Father's Spirit, so long asked for, is given; the victory over sin, so long sought for, is found of a sudden; the gate of righteousness, knocked at so perseveringly, opens to the waiting feet: and another pure-hearted son of God, bright with the image of his Father, and made like unto the Christ, enters the radiant city of the crowned and perfected!

PART II.
SECOND RELATION TO EVIL.

II. Many who care little for other portions of our Lord's teaching are fond of quoting the pithy portable rule about neighbourly conduct between man and man which follows on His persuasive to prayer. Unlike the peculiar doctrines of the gospel, this appears to lie level to the moral perceptions of even worldly-hearted persons; it affords them a handy test by which to expose practical inconsistencies in the religious; and, as we are all ready to select from Scripture those parts which please us best, so you find this to be a favourite text with people who hardly pretend to be devout or spiritual, but flatter themselves that they do better to stick to such homely week-day duties as every one can understand. Hence this

Ver. 12.

has come to be popularly looked upon as the very key to the ethics of Christ, the most original and characteristic maxim of His law: an exaggeration which has naturally provoked equally unfair efforts on the other side to depreciate both the value and the originality of this so-called 'golden rule.' The abruptness also of its introduction, its apparent want of relation to the sentences which here precede and follow it, and the fact that in St. Luke's report it is introduced at a much earlier passage of the Sermon, have cast some doubts upon the place which really belongs to it in Jesus' exposition of His Kingdom.

First, then, as to its *connection* with the foregoing. A sentence introduced with the word 'therefore' naturally points us to the immediately preceding passage for its ground. The immediately preceding passage has enforced with all possible urgency the duty of believing and persevering prayer, on the ground that God, as our heavenly Father, will certainly bestow every 'good gift' which His children need. It seems an obvious enough inference, that because God is ever ready to hear and help us when we call, 'therefore' the most difficult duties of unselfish brother-love to men become possible for us. This rule of doing to others as we should like them to

Of Escaping the World's Evil. 139

do to us, is evidently meant to be a convenient short-hand expression for all the relative duties of society. So much is plain from the words: 'This is the law and the prophets.' It is a summary, therefore, of whatever our Lord has taught throughout this whole discourse respecting that righteousness of perfect love betwixt man and man, which exceeds the righteousness of Hebrew scribe or Pharisee. Possibly even the form of this phrase, 'the law and the prophets,' may allude to the similar language with which He had begun His exposition of christian righteousness, near the outset of His discourse. But we do not need on that account to stretch the reference of His 'therefore' so far back. The whole of this lofty righteousness to which Jesus has been binding His disciples, with its spirit of love and its godlike perfectness of motive, becomes what it never was before, a possible, attainable thing, even for 'evil' men, so soon as we firmly grasp the power of persevering petition, or the hold which Christ, the Reconciler of His brethren, gives to us as God's children over our great Parent's heart. He who knows the Father as this Son has now discovered Him, and has leave to ask confidently for every good and needful gift, need not despair of keeping even this law. For it is thus that 'the

PART II.

SECOND
RELATION TO
EVIL.

See v. 17.

As Meyer, *e.g.*, does, *in loc.*

Ver. 11.

righteousness of the law' comes to be 'fulfilled in us who walk no longer after the flesh, but after' that Holy 'Spirit' Whom the Father gives to His recovered children. In vain, therefore, shall any still unreconciled and unregenerate reader of this divine discourse wrench this 'golden rule' of neighbourliness out of its vital connection with the new relation in which Christ sets men to God, and with the inner life of prayer, and with the gift of the Holy Ghost. In vain shall it be cited as a dislocated moral maxim, such as might have dropped from a Hebrew or a Pagan teacher: for then, cut off from the spirit of christian life and the childlike fellowship of the redeemed with their Father, its strength goes from it; it becomes weak like any other lovely but dead word of the moralists, a word to be admired but never practised.

So also of the *originality* of this 'golden rule.' Expressed in a negative form: 'Do not to another what you dislike when done to yourself,' it is far from original. We find it in the Jewish Apocrypha; we find it among the sayings of the Rabbis; we find it, as Gibbon reminds us with a sneer, in a Greek moralist 'four hundred years before the publication of the gospel.'[1] It is true

---

[1] See Tobit iv. 16: 'Do that to no man which thou hatest'

Of Escaping the World's Evil. 141

that this negative form of the rule falls immensely beneath the positive; since it is, of course, a vastly higher effort of charity to do to our neighbour every possible act of kindness, than simply to abstain from any express act of injury. But though this positive reading of the maxim by our Lord is (so far as I know) original in its form, yet it is, after all, nothing else but a new way of putting the very old command in which the Mosaic law had summed up its second table: 'Thou shalt love thy neighbour as thyself.' If I put my neighbour and myself on the same level of affection—God only being raised above it—then I shall not wish more good to myself than I wish to him; that is to say, I shall not expect him to do for me any kindness which I am not equally prepared to do for him in like circumstances. This is just our 'golden rule.' The fact is, Jesus never claimed originality for any part of His moral teaching, but was always at pains to indicate how, substantially, it all lay *in gremio* within the envelope of the older economy, and needed only to be unfolded in the spirit of it in order to blossom into the full and (cf. Ecclus. xxxi. 15); cited as a saying of Rabbi Hillel by the Talmud, as Wetstein and other commentators note. The Greek parallel from Isocrates is quoted by Gibbon in *Decline and Fall* (ch. 54, note 36).

PART II.

SECOND RELATION TO EVIL.

Lev. xix. 18. See *Laws of the Kingdom*, p. 112.

PART II.
SECOND
RELATION TO
EVIL.

perfect loveliness of New Testament ethics. What was absolutely original in the gospel and is to this day unrivalled, is, that it professes to set sinful men into such a new relation to God, that they can draw down from Him by devout acts of desire a divine influence potent enough to fulfil within them that ethical and spiritual ideal of human duty, which all ancient codes more or less recognised, but utterly failed to realize. The morals of Christianity are the least novel or characteristic portion of its teaching: yet we cannot say they are its least important. You do not speak of degrees of importance among the parts of a tree. The root exists for the sake of the flower and seed; but flower and seed do not come without the root. The doctrines of the christian gospel are that root out of which christian graces bloom and christian fruits are scattered over the waste lands; but it is no less thankless than foolish work to cut the tree asunder.

What, then, in the last place, is the *design* with which, at the present stage of His discourse, Jesus has introduced this *resumé* of brotherly love ? Only, as I think, for a handy defence against that unbrotherly style of retaliation into which contact with the world's evil is so apt to

Of Escaping the World's Evil. 143

betray His disciples. It is the Christian in his inevitable contest with an enveloping society of unchristian and wicked men, whom throughout this section our Saviour appears to have in view. His words take the form of plain practical hints, how he who would overcome evil, instead of being overcome by it, must behave himself. The fundamental rule is to live by prayer: to fall back on divine help: to keep open that secret avenue of access to the unseen Father, which is like the communication of a general, hardly beset, with his source of supplies. But just because the disciple has such stores of supernatural aid within reach, is it practicable for him to retaliate upon the world's evil, not with evil, but with good. If the Christian suffer his behaviour towards bad men to become a reflection of their behaviour towards him—if he does to others what they do to him—he forfeits his superior and exceptional character as a child of God. So far from assimilating the world to himself, he will grow assimilated to it. This is always a near and pressing danger. For when the world uses a Christian ill, all the evil within his heart will rise up as at a bugle-note of defiance, and claim to be allowed to pay men back in their own coin. There is even a sophistical look of even-handedness about this

PART II.
SECOND
RELATION TO
EVIL.

Vers. 7–11.

which pleads plausibly. 'Why should I not do to others what they do to me?' Simply for this reason, that you are—what they are not—a child of the Father in heaven. You are bound, therefore, to act, not like evil men, but like the good God, making His example, and not theirs, your model. Moreover, you are able to practise this divine species of retribution, however much it may go against nature, because it is not you only who act, but the Spirit of your Father Who acteth in you. It is not, then, what men give us which is to measure our return to them, but what they ought to give; not what they have done, but what we instinctively wish they had done. The sentence contains, not an ethical principle, but a popular rule. Such measuring of one's duty by one's self-love is like a pocket-standard, always at hand and prompt of application; of special utility, therefore, in those sudden emergencies which are constantly occurring, in which a child of God is called to act swiftly and alone amid the press of this world's selfish society. It is very difficult to be always unlike other men; to meet barefaced injury with divine returns; to get the world's treatment of us measured out of one dish, and give it back out of a quite different one. It needs prayer in the

Margin notes: PART II. SECOND RELATION TO EVIL. Cf. Matt. x. 20.

closet, indeed, first of all; but it also needs in the market-place some serviceable memorable rule, adjusted to the golden standard of heaven, yet of ready application in the affairs of earth. Such a rule is this: Do as you would be done by.

PART II.

SECOND RELATION TO EVIL.

III. Neither the gracious assurance of divine aid to be had for earnest asking, nor this most serviceable of practical guides to right action, can make the christian life an easy one. No disciple, indeed, has occasion for despair, with God at hand to be importuned; but as little can he afford, in a world like this, to be indolent or self-indulgent. Divine grace is promised to the prayerful, not to supersede the call for personal effort or painful self-denial, but, on the contrary, to brace the soul for that stern and resolute pursuit of singular holiness, without which the gates of the Kingdom may be set ever so open to all comers, yet set open to us in vain. Nor is that intercourse with the world which provokes a Christian to weigh his conduct in the world's own measure, instead of returning good for its evil, to be an intercourse without limits. The world's way and his way are different. Christ was no ascetic, as John was: still there is, after all, a certain christian discipline which is of

Vers. 13, 14.

PART II.
SECOND
RELATION TO
EVIL.

kin to asceticism. Some self-imposed singularity, an avoidance of the ways of the pleasure-loving crowd, and a soldier-like choice of labour and hardship; these things have their place in the christian ideal, and must be elected by him who would win his way upward to the christian heaven. Were we invited to be holy amid a society of holy ones, where every surrounding influence told in favour of goodness, and the sympathy of our comrades came to the aid of our own faltering virtue, the task of christian service would still be a self-displeasing task, painful to nature, and involving violence to tastes and passions which are hard to be subdued. So those devotees have found, who in evil times have striven to create for themselves a better world within the world, a safer and more guarded society, where, under less arduous conditions, the individual Christian might prosecute this needful labour of self-mortification, and, hand in hand with a like-minded few, might climb the steeps of purity and devotion. But such a resource, whatever be its value, is not open to us. It is in the midst of this world's society, not out of it, that we must learn to be unworldly; and the difficulty of prosecuting inwardly and secretly a course of exceptional self-discipline, while outwardly forming part of

John xvii. 15.

the vast, gay, various, fascinating, entangling scene which we call 'the world,' is a difficulty which it is hardly possible to overstate. To mark out for one's self an uphill path of effort when the descent to Avernus is so easy; to keep straight on with stedfast purpose, though byways of delight allure on either hand; to walk with wary foot the narrow ledge of duty, where one false step may prove a fatal one; to dare to go alone, God only for unseen Approver, nor heed the mockery of the crowd who flout and pity us: this is that course of life, wholesome in its severity, and rough with self-elected pains, to which the solemn voice of our King has called His followers.

<small>PART II.

SECOND RELATION TO EVIL.

Facilis descensus Averni.</small>

I suppose this figuring of man's life as a path wherein we go is as old as the life of man. The aged Jacob described his 'few and evil' years to Pharaoh as a 'pilgrimage;' and the confession of thoughtful men from the beginning has been, that here on the earth they were only travellers in a strange land, passing on to an unknown home beyond. Nor is the choice of paths a less familiar image in all literature for the momentous moral decision which faces every comer into life. The 'strange woman' of the Proverbs, in whose paths of flattery and death 'many strong men

<small>Gen. xlvii. 9.

Cf. Heb. xi. 13–16; c. 1 Chron. xxix. 15.

See Prov. vii.–ix. *passim.*</small>

have been slain,' with the contrasted figure of Wisdom, whose voice in the 'places of the paths' finds few to hearken as she calls men all day long to 'keep her ways,' that conduct to life and health: this inspired parable of the Hebrews has its close counterpart in the classical legend of young Hercules, solicited at the outset of life by seductive pleasure on the one hand, and on the other by wise and noble self-control. It is an old, old moral. Still before the tender feet of each new generation, as it stands in the pride of an untried freedom at the parting of the ways, there stretch these two divergent paths,—the pleasant flowery road the unseen end of which is destruction, and that unpromising mountain-path whose roughness and narrowness conduct the resolute wayfarer to life. Still by the youth's side there stand two rival persuaders, such as Leonardo has fixed for us on his teaching canvas: Venus and Minerva; L'Allegro and Il Penseroso: the loose patron of pleasure, with languishing eye, and voice of promise sweet to the credulous ear of youth; and on the other side, unadorned grave wisdom, draped in sober grey, whose words speak only to the ear of faith, call only to a manhood of hardness, and keep their promises for the far-off to come.

A closer parallel than any of these, and, I

think, the closest to be found to the form of our
Lord's parable, is that exquisite passage in the
Second Book of Esdras, in which the inheritance
prepared for God's chosen is set forth as a city
'set upon a broad field,' and 'full of all good
things;' but it has only a single entrance, and
that a strait one, the 'one only' access to which
is by a path so narrow, 'that there could but one
man go there at once,' and running along a
perilous passage with 'fire on the right hand, and
on the left a deep water.' The moral of the
passage is, that if God's Israel, for whom so much
has been done, will not be at pains to suffer now
'the strait commandment' of God in 'hope of
wide things' to come, 'they can never receive
what is laid up for them.' The resemblance of
this allegory and its moral to our Lord's must
strike every reader; the main difference being
that, in our Lord's, the broad path, which is the
converse of the narrow one trodden by few, is
made equally distinct, and the contrast thereby
brought out in fuller relief and with unmatched
impressiveness. On the other hand, it is not so
clear whether our Lord desires us to think of the
gate as standing at the beginning or at the end
of the way. In the one case, two roads of life
will be viewed as leading us all towards one or

PART II.

SECOND
RELATION TO
EVIL.

See 2 Esdras
vii. 6–25.

other of two entrances, whose folding-doors admit the wayfarer either to the dark metropolis of evil, the prison-city of destruction, or to that capital seat of blessedness and honour, the celestial city of God. This reading corresponds with the Esdras parallel, and with many familiar representations in Holy Scripture. But our Lord's repeated mention of the gate *before* the way seems almost to shut us up[1] to a different form of the figure. We may think, if we will, of human travellers as starting together from one enclosed place with a double outlet. The great gate stands always open, choked with a throng who press through its inviting portals to find outside a spacious avenue, bordered with delights, having devious tracks traversing it, and broadening at intervals into still ampler spaces that allure to repose. Somewhere in the wall there is a small unpromising wicket, which affords an alternative egress; but there are few who notice it, or care to seek for it, or will wait and knock at its shut door; and those who do find outside only a very narrow and rugged[2] hill track, which pre-

Marginal notes: PART II. SECOND RELATION TO EVIL. — εὔχωρος, lit. 'broad-spaced.'

---

[1] With Bengel, Lange, Meyer, and some others, though not the majority of expositors.

[2] The word 'narrow' (τεθλιμμένη) applied to the 'way' (v. 14) is taken by some to mean 'rough.' Literally, it means 'close-pressed.'

Of Escaping the World's Evil. 151

sently leads them up from the soft valley into a mountain region where the hardiest must walk with circumspection, for the cliffs press them on the right and the chasm yawns upon the left; a region lonely and full of perils, pierced by a path arduous to climb and painful to tread. Only that pleasant frequented road has 'destruction' for its termination; it is this mountain track which conducts us up to 'life' and God.

So Jesus left His figure: a figure too plain to need interpretation. So, with a terrible sadness which wastes no words, He warns us from the way of death, and urges us to seek with an urgency winged by fear His own blood-sprinkled path. The earnestness of One Who died as well as spoke for our salvation burns through these sentences. No one who has followed this Preacher of the Kingdom through the previous paragraphs of this Sermon, with a soul braced in good earnest to do all His bidding, will feel at all surprised to hear Him term the path of new evangelical obedience a 'strait' path. So straitly is it fenced to right and left by prescriptions too exacting for human virtue, so rough is it with flinty duties reluctantly undertaken by any selfish or easy heart, that, after we have weighed well the privileges of God's christian children, and the

PART II.
———
SECOND
RELATION TO
EVIL.

Mf. v. 21 ff.

large promises made to prayer, and the splendid rewards laid up in the hereafter, we have still need to gird ourselves with patient resolution, as men do for a long and solitary and discouraging march. Only we have no option, if we would have life. Divine eyes looked abroad across the manifold lines of human action and into the tangled characters and aims of this world's society, before He thus sharply sundered all the motley throngs who pass along such diverse paths through life into two—and no more than two—classes. Divine eyes had pierced to the radical secret of character, found the key to man's fate, and foreseen the ultimate judgment which is to sort us all in the end according to our works, before He could thus confidently pronounce upon the issues of such ambiguous lives as men lead here below. Jesus certainly does not speak in this place after a human fashion. To us, the paths of men seem endless in their moral diversity: who feels himself fit to part his brothers betwixt heaven and hell? To Jesus, the roads we go and the ends we reach have a divine simplicity: they are but two; and He enunciates them with a divine certainty: destruction or life. No option is left us, therefore. To flinch from the road of christian obedience, because of its narrow limits and severe demands upon us, is to perish.

It is true that this difficulty of christian service is precisely that which deters the mass of men from entering upon it. The world has a deal to offer to him who will go after it. Its fields are green, its paths are soft, its flowers are fair, its fruits are sweet. It fills the air with song, it beats the earth with dancing feet, it knows to while the tedious hours away with dalliance and laughter. It will make work that must be done as light as it can be made, and fill up intervals of leisure with pleasures which banish thought. Or should the graver cares of study or ambition be your preference, you may choose your own path—so long as it is your own. For, amid the endless varieties to be found in life's broad road, there is but this single mark by which to recognise all travellers: they take the path which seems right in their own eyes. And the repulsiveness of christian living is accordingly to be sought just here, in its requiring us to deny our likings that we may go the way, and hear the voice, and do the bidding, of Another, in our own despite. Is it strange if comparatively few go out of their path to seek for, and with pains and self-denial press their steps into, so confined a way through a gate of straitness?

But then, on the other hand, this very unpopularity of christian life increases its difficulty. To deny one's own likings in order to serve Christ is not easy at the best: it is doubly hard when to do it you must incur the pain of being singular. On another occasion, when Jesus was asked, in a spirit of idle curiosity, whether there are few that be saved, He gave, in place of a direct reply, only this same exhortation to be in earnest about one's personal salvation; He sharpened His words to a still keener edge: 'Agonize to go in at the strait gate;' and He enforced His admonition by the warning that, of those who do seek to enter, 'many shall not be able.' Even from that passage one might gather that our Lord did not anticipate that the number of His genuine and loyal followers should ever preponderate in the world. In this passage He surely says so expressly. To Him, those who were to receive the Kingdom were ever a 'little flock;' and the history of Christendom has been a running illustration of His words. Even when the deepest and on the whole strongest currents determining the great movements of secular history have obeyed a christian impulse,— as, for example, when the Roman Empire turned from Paganism to Christianity, or when the sixteenth century Reformation determined in the seventeenth the wars and alliances of Europe,—those individuals who genuinely sought to obey the laws of Jesus have never been in a majority. The world of society is still, in spite of all, a broad road, where a thousand preferences lead men after a thousand interests, and you may humour any whim or chase any phantom delight you please, but where those are few and far between who thoroughly subordinate everything else to the one end of obeying, copying, and pleasing as their King and Leader, the Lord Jesus Christ. Those who do, find their christian career made immensely more difficult by such singularity. The mass of one's neighbours is huge enough to generate a public opinion against which it is hard to contend. Among the crowds who affect no christian isolation or peculiarity, there are so many whom on other grounds one must love and venerate, that it is hard always to feel sure that one is right and they all wrong. So much which is innocuous, desirable, and excellent is mixed up, through this disastrous condition of society at large, with the mighty current sweeping downwards away from Christ, and must be abandoned along with it, that one resents the sacrifice as if the world had robbed us of a part of our patrimony. When the good cannot be disentangled from the evil, both have to be thrown away together; and perforce to throw away a good thing is bitter loss. To sensitive natures with a broad humanity, there is even, at the root of all this, a fixed pain in being profoundly out of harmony with the bulk of their fellow-men. Not mainly through dread of being ridiculed. That is possibly a ruder trouble, though it certainly besets fine natures. At any rate, the isolation of the true Christian is in our age more an inward than an outward isolation. Usually it involves no avoidance of common life, save of such doubtful or disreputable scenes as any man may avoid without being singular. There is nothing to hinder any one from living the severest life of christian self-discipline and restraint, or devoting one's self under the noblest motives to christian service, without abandoning society, or even continuing to attract exceptional remark. For the secret aim of life may be entirely controlled by Christ's law under a strict observance of His restraints, while the outer life is not obtrusively changed. But, with all this, many tender souls will be painfully aware that they have in all grave affairs parted company

Of Escaping the World's Evil. 157

from their neighbours and acquaintances. Having put their life docilely into the hand of Christ, He seems to lead them up out of their old sympathies with common life, into a lonely place whose keener air others do not breathe, and the hardships of which hardly a soul knows but themselves,—a height to which the din of earthly interests appears to rise faint and far off like the hum of a remoter land.

After all, it is, in the heart and secret history of it, a singular march for the golden city to each separate pilgrim. Spiritual discipline in the secret following of Christ is (as that Book of Esdras describes it) a pathway where two cannot walk quite abreast. Alone, each of us must seek that small wicket-door which stands at the head of the way, and by a solitary repentance set out for heaven. Alone, too, each one must deal with the exceptional defects and faults of his own character—must train himself by solitary self-examination, prayer, and denial. The eye of each must be on the One Forerunner Whose shining prints attest to the heedful looker that our feet are keeping the narrow path; and when we wander or grow faint, it is by a cry which only His ear catches that we have to summon to our aid the unseen Hand of His help. Who knows,

PART II.
SECOND
RELATION TO
EVIL.

See Ps. xxiv.

save Him, our falls and risings, our stumbles and toils? Who, save Him, shall see when alone the weary pilgrim reaches home at last and enters in, not, as at the first, by the strait wicket of a humbling penitence, but at the mighty golden gates of Jehovah's Temple—those 'everlasting doors' through which the clean of hand and pure of heart shall pass, to stand for ever beside the King of Glory within His holy place?

OF DETECTING FALSE TEACHERS
IN THE KINGDOM.

Beware of false prophets, which come to you in sheep's clothing, but inwardly they are ravening wolves. Ye shall know them by their fruits. Do men gather grapes of thorns, or figs of thistles? Even so every good tree bringeth forth good fruit; but a corrupt tree bringeth forth evil fruit. A good tree cannot bring forth evil fruit, neither can a corrupt tree bring forth good fruit. Every tree that bringeth not forth good fruit is hewn down, and cast into the fire. Wherefore by their fruits ye shall know them.—MATT. VII. 15-20. Cf. LUKE VI. 43-45.

OF DETECTING FALSE TEACHERS IN THE KINGDOM.

THE way to life, being narrow, is ill to find. It is therefore found by few; and he who would walk in it must make up his mind to walk alone against a mighty crowd that presses the other way. To follow Christ means to withstand the world's example. But this is not all. There are never wanting would-be guides, who volunteer to show to seeking souls the path of life; smooth-tongued teachers, who beset the steps of the credulous pilgrim, and, under professions of unusual interest in his salvation, counsel him to select a less arduous road to heaven. A new peril thus attends the christian disciple. To that danger which arises from the existence of God's little kingdom within this vast and evil world of the ungodly, there comes another danger from the existence of evil and worldly elements within God's kingdom itself. This danger, too, is all the greater, because such evil as creeps into the fold of Christ to mislead

PART II.

THIRD RELATION TO EVIL.

His followers, must disguise itself. Out in the open world you see the crowds who plod or gambol down to death, making no concealment of their sin. But when evil enters the enclosed and guarded kingdom of Christ's saints, it must wear a specious cloak of goodness and speak the language of the kingdom. Only under pretence of conducting men to eternal life, can such deceivers betray them to eternal death.

The transition which our Lord here makes from the last to the present paragraph, is accordingly one of contrast. From the relations of His christian society to the world of open evil outside of it, He passes to its relations to such evil as may lurk inside of it.[1] Now it is exceedingly significant that our Lord represents the evil which was sure to penetrate within His Church, and which has so largely succeeded in secularizing it, as commencing from false teachers. At the outset, His followers may be assumed to be all of them men who are sincere in seeking a way to celestial life. Who would attach himself to this lowly and rejected Master for any other reason? But when the conditions which

---

[1] The Church in the evil world is like 'sheep in the midst of wolves' (Matt. x. 16); conversely, the world within the Church is like wolves among the sheep (vii. 15). On the use of this emblem, cf. Ecclus. xiii. 17.

He lays down are discovered to be so stringent, and the path He leads in so strait and steep, it presently begins to be said, or imagined, that life may be had on easier terms. The original gospel of the King undergoes some modification. Surreptitiously, corruption of doctrine enters. Teachers who profess to teach still in the name of Jesus, point men to a path which looks deceptively like the narrow way, and appears to conduct to a similar issue; only it is not so narrow, after all, as the narrow way itself, and in the end its issues are not really different from those of the broad road that leads to death. Now, it is plain that corruption of doctrine which begins thus, must end in corruption of morals. The very *motif* to such false teaching is a desire to broaden somewhat the excessive straitness of the gospel path to life, to relax a little the ethical severity of Christ's kingdom; and however such a *motif* may in the first instance conceal itself, it cannot fail in the long run to work its natural fruit in a lower standard of christian behaviour, and some concession to the evil world. False teaching of Christianity, therefore, ends in making false Christians: a process quite faithfully reflected in this closing portion of our Lord's sermon. From a warning against

PART II.

THIRD RELATION TO EVIL.

Cf. ver. 15 with ver. 23.

pseudo-prophets, the Preacher advances by an almost insensible transition to the doom of professors who work iniquity.

For the same reason, it lies deep in the nature of the case that the ultimate test of all teaching which calls itself christian can only be its moral tendency and results. Such a test was of especial value in the first age of Christianity, before the formation and acceptance of the New Testament canon had furnished the Church with an unchanging literary standard of truth. Even amid the confused and contradictory deductions which have in later Christendom been drawn from the words of Scripture, this practical criterion remains as an invaluable check upon our mistakes of interpretation. Its ground lies here: 'The Son of God was manifested, that He might destroy the works of the devil.' His gospel has for its practical end to deliver men from sin, and reproduce within them the likeness of their Father in heaven. It follows, that whatever does not really contribute towards this moral process, or, at least, whatever is found practically to tell in an opposite direction, can be no portion of genuine gospel teaching. It would have been well if theologians had always kept more steadily before their view that it is this ethical design to lead men in the way of holiness which constitutes the very *raison d'être* of the christian system, and that no branch of christian doctrine may decline to be tried by its manifest results on human life.

What I have now said, however, though it is a fair deduction from His words, is not the same thing as our Lord says in the text. To judge of doctrines by their ultimate ethical results upon society is one thing; to judge of them by the personal conduct of those who preach them is quite another. It has sometimes happened in the history of heresies, that a serious and in the end disastrous aberration from sound doctrine was broached for the first time by a man of unimpeachable sincerity and christian pureness of living. It is not to teachers of this class that Jesus points, at least in terms: though here also the principle of judgment on which He proceeds admits of a valid, though less immediate, application; an application not to the original teacher, but to the system taught. The class of false teachers which Jesus evidently had in His eye[1] embraced such as were either intentional

---

[1] Cf. the use of οἵτινες in ver. 15 = 'teachers of such a sort as come in sheep's clothing,' etc.

PART II.
THIRD
LATION TO
EVIL.

deceivers, misguiding the Church through evil will, and stealing into her communion under false colours, with a fixed purpose to delude the unwary; or (which is more probable) men who taught a false gospel, because, in their own spiritual darkness of heart, they had never themselves repented unto life, nor ever found for their own salvation that true way of peace which they professed to indicate to others. In both cases, unquestionably, false doctrine will be a direct product of an unrenewed and, at its core, evil heart. Grant only sufficient time for the full development of character, and the radically unchristian spirit of teachers of this stamp may be expected to display itself in flagrantly unchristian lives.

Now, that the Preacher spoke so personally, and restricted the application of His moral test to the character of individual teachers, came in part from the concrete manner which was characteristic of Him. Jesus left it to the subsequent reflection of His Church to think out those principles which always underlay His utterances, and to apply them afresh to new occasions as the need arose. For Himself, He usually threw His lessons into some popular form, bearing immediately upon the case before Him, and easily intelligible by His first hearers.

Of Detecting False Teachers in the Kingdom. 167

Here, for instance, when He spoke of false prophets who, underneath a sheep's skin, concealed the disposition of a wolf, His Jewish audience could be at no loss to understand the kind of teachers He meant. They were only too familiar with religious rulers of their own nation and expositors of their own Scriptures, whose sanctimonious exterior concealed the vices of a hypocrite; who, as Jesus on a later occasion described them at Jerusalem, in words which recall the vigorous denunciations of Ezekiel, were no true shepherds, but 'thieves and robbers' who had climbed into God's fold, that, under pretence of herding, they might ravage and plunder it. Of such false and wicked teachers among the Pharisees of His own day, Jesus was not now speaking, it is true;[1] but He was speaking of false and wicked teachers very similar to them in character and mode of operation, who should within a very short time find their way into His own infant kingdom. His words are certainly prophetic; but they describe a state of matters in the New Testament Church very like

PART II.

THIRD RELATION TO EVIL.

John x. 1–10; cf. Ezek. xxxiv.

---

[1] Neither can He be taken as alluding here to false pretenders to Messiahship, whose appearance before the fall of Jerusalem is predicted in Matt. xxiv. 24. But the reference (see xxiv. 11) earlier in the same discourse may be to the heretics of the early Church, as in the text before us.

PART II.
THIRD
RELATION TO
EVIL.

what His hearers had before their eyes in the Old Testament commonwealth; and the state of matters which He so vividly forecast came to pass at no distant date. The early history of Christianity furnishes a full justification of the form into which our Lord threw His warning. Those very men to whom He mainly addressed this sermon—the new-made apostles—were not yet in their graves before such an irruption of evil doctrine as is here foretold, alarmed the leaders of the Church in every part of Christendom. Again and again the language of the apostolic letters reflects these forewarning words of the Founder. When St. Paul, indeed, speaking at Miletus in the spring of 58, alluded to these very words of his Lord, it was still only to warn the Ephesian elders both against 'grievous wolves' who should come from without the Church, and against 'perverse' men who should arise within it. But the evil which had not then reached Ephesus was already at work in Corinth and Galatia; for, writing to these churches in the previous year, he had denounced the 'pseudo-apostles' and 'pseudo-brethren,' who had crept in under false appearances,[1] as servants

Acts xx. 29, 30;
for the date,
see Wieseler,
Chron. d. apost.
Zeitalters.

Cor. xi. 13–
; Gal. ii. 4,
Greek.

---

[1] Our Lord's phrase about 'sheep's clothing' finds its best commentary in what St. Paul wrote (in the same year 57) to

of Satan, whose end should be as their works were. The letters to Titus and Timothy probably belong to a later date; and by that time we find heretical leaders infesting the Church not only at Ephesus, as Paul had foreseen, but in Crete also. The false teaching had its roots in the evil heart, and it led to evil practices. Some, having put away a good conscience, had in consequence made shipwreck of their faith; others, who failed to keep love in view as the end of the law, had turned aside to 'vain jangling' in doctrine. Deceitful talkers were thus subverting whole households for the sake of gain —their words eating as a canker into the life of the Church; and many of the brethren had been like men who, after being drugged, were entrapped alive in the nets of Satan. Still worse and more perilous times he saw impending on the christian world. Nor was St. Paul mistaken in his dark auguries. The diabolical doctrines of which he forewarned the Church, and the wicked seducers whom he expected to 'wax worse and worse,' are fully matched by the 'damnable heresies' of profligate and presumptuous apostates, so vehe-

PART II.

THIRD RELATION TO EVIL.

See 1 Tim. i. 3; Tit. i. 5.

Cf. 1 Cor. xv. 33.

1 Tim. i. 19.

Ibid. ver. 6.

Tit. i. 10, 11; c. 2 Tim. ii. 17.

2 Tim. ii. 26, Greek; cf. iii. 8.

See 1 Tim. iv. 1 ff.; 2 Tim. iii. 1-5, 13.

Cf. 2 Pet. ii. and Jude, *pass.*

Rome about men who for sensual ends 'deceive the hearts of the simple' by 'good words and fair speeches:' see Rom. xvi. 17–20 (cf. 'having a form of godliness, but denying the power thereof,' in 2 Tim. iii. 5).

mently inveighed against by St. Peter and St. Jude. And finally, before St. John left the world, heresies which he did not hesitate to brand as antichristian were promulgated by men against whom he bade his converts close their doors. The whole apostolical literature, in fact, proves that, within half a century after Jesus uttered this warning, every portion of His infant Church was literally overrun with false teachers of precisely the description here drawn; men who under the garb of Christians covered the same vices of rapacity, profligacy, and guile which had made a section of the Pharisaic party infamous; men whose misleading doctrines sprang secretly from an evil heart, and were shown to be false by their practical results in an evil life.

Such was the pertinence of Jesus' warning to His first followers; and the test He gave them was both a practicable and a trustworthy one. Men who 'turn the grace of our God into lasciviousness,' are men who really walk, not in the narrow, but in the broad way, while they allure others into it on pretence that it is the way to life. To learn the true nature of such men, you have to look not at their external profession, which is a thing put on, but at their real behaviour, which is a genuine outcome of the life within. Two metaphors are employed; but in passing from the sheep-skin hanging on the wolf's back to the fruit growing on a living plant, it is obvious that Jesus sets in contrast that part of a man's visible life which has a radical or vital connection with his own nature, over against that other part which has no such connection at all. Suppose you stay by the first metaphor alone; then the meaning would be expressed thus: The wolf in sheep-skin is detected for a wolf as soon as it begins to ravin. Or, express it wholly under the second figure, and it will run thus: The buckthorn is not a vine, because the bunches of black berries on its tall stalk may look so like grapes as to cheat the distant eye: taste them; they are but bitter and unwholesome after all.[1] The first metaphor is best adapted to convey the idea of an assumed or ungenuine exterior, a behaviour which belongs to good men simulated by the bad. The second is most fit to carry this thought, that the real, not assumed, behaviour of every man must be a faithful expression of his inner life, and therefore the ultimate

PART II.

THIRD RELATION TO EVIL.

Cf. Tholuck, *in loc.*

---

[1] In St. James' use of the figure (iii. 12), the difference between good and useless fruits disappears. The botanical emblem is with him subordinate to another figure (that of water, briny or sweet, from a fountain) by which the same idea is expressed.

index by which character is judged. Combine the lessons of both, and you have a vivid picture of the danger of judging solely by appearances, which may be assumed, and the necessity of verifying such appearances by the genuine outcome of character in practice.

With this clue in our hand, we shall hardly misread the meaning of our Lord. Two readings certainly are possible. Ever since men began to study the Gospels, a difference of opinion has prevailed on the point whether the 'fruits' by which the false prophets are to be known denote their personal conduct or their doctrines.[1] Now,

[1] To us it does seem inconceivable how the bulk both of the early Fathers, and of the reformed divines before Bengel, could take our Lord as meaning that we are to detect false teachers by the falseness of their teaching. Is not that to assume the very thing which has to be decided? It is true that there is, as has been said, a class of heretical or mistaken teachers, whose lives are pure though their creed may in some things be heterodox; and therefore our Lord's words will not bear to be pressed further than the limitations of the case warrant: but it was surely making too much of orthodoxy to say (even in a 'Catholic' age) that all mistaken theologians must be 'hewn down and cast into the fire.' The 'fruits' of such a misconception have been only too patent and too unhappy. Nearly every commentator who has read the test in this way has turned it against those in the Church whose views of doctrine differed from his own. The Fathers directed its edge against all sects outside the Catholic Church; Maldonatus against the Calvinists; Calvinists against the Socinians. The weapon is too perilous a one to be wielded in this fashion. Fortunately, it cuts all ways; and such opposite applications refute one another.

to us it appears that the first key to a judicious interpretation of the text must lie in its immediate limitation to a certain foreseen description of errorists; to such as should deliberately pervert the gospel in the interests of a relaxed moral code and a more or less impure life. So applied, the test of conduct is obviously in its place. The false teaching is convicted of being false by its vital connection with the evil life of the teacher. The second key lies in the distinction betwixt such outward behaviour as may be assumed, and such as must be a genuine product of a man's nature. It is not accurate to say that the distinction lies betwixt words and acts. The cloak assumed by a hypocrite often lies quite as much in borrowed actions as in borrowed language: he does what he sees good men do, as well as says what he hears them say. On the other hand, words when unstudied are to the full as faithful a reflex of character as deeds, because a more rapid or impromptu utterance of it.[1] The real

[1] Hence in Luke's parallel report (vi. 45) we find words inserted which imply that a man's words are the 'fruit' by which he is to be known. This parallel has no doubt assisted to confuse interpreters. But the good or evil which a man's mouth speaketh must come from the abundance, literally, the overflow (περίσσευμα) of his heart or real moral life, if it is to be a genuine fruit by which he can be judged. (The same idea under the same image recurs in a different connection in Matt. xii. 33.)

contrast is between the affected and the spontaneous exhibitions of character; what a man pretends to be when he is acting a part, and what he betrays himself to be when he acts naturally. Here again, of course, genuine conduct may be fitly appealed to, in order to test such conduct as may or may not be genuine. From the evidence of a man's dress, an appeal always lies to the better evidence of his life.

At the same time, it is obvious that the principle of detection laid down in these verses is one for all time. When our Lord puts us to school among the shrubs, and bids us note how absolute is the law by which each species bears only its own proper fruit, according to its kind,—nay, how the inward soundness or decay of each plant, even within the same species, betrays itself in the quality of its fruit,—He lays to our hand a canon of judgment whose sweep is a great deal wider than the occasion before Him. We may not always be able to detect teachers of error, as He bade His apostles detect the 'deceitful workers' of the first century. In an age like ours, an age of spiritual restlessness, yet, on the whole, of honest search after truth, when the indirect moral influence of the gospel goes far beyond the limits of its dogmatic acceptance, we see on every hand of us the poorest of creeds, and even the deadliest of doctrines, advocated by plausible men of upright motives and blameless conduct. We live amid a din of opinion, more diverse in speech than Babel, where every sectary vaunts his peculiar creed, and every self-styled instructor or 'prophet' of men claims to possess the infallible *recipé* for a blessed life; and though we cannot apply our King's test after the rough and ready fashion of the early age, we do sorely need some sovereign touchstone, if we could but find one, to detect false teaching by, however smooth or sincere may be the lips that speak it. Now, apart from a direct appeal to the unequivocal testimony of God speaking to us through His sacred Scriptures,[1] when such is to be had, there is no other criterion half so safe or reliable as an appeal to moral results. Systems of philosophy, schemes for political regeneration, and all degrees of belief or of no belief in religion which people embrace, underlie the operation of this natural law quite as surely as does individual character. Every doctrine, true

---

[1] 'To the Law and to the Testimony! If they speak not according to this Word, it is because there is no light in them' (Isa. viii. 20).

PART II.
THIRD
RELATION TO
EVIL.

or false, which a man really accepts and lives by, translates itself sooner or later into practice; and the quality of the practice to which it leads is a perfectly fair index to the worth or goodness of the doctrine. Nothing can be God's truth which, fairly acted out, is found in the long run and on a sufficient induction of instances to lead to sin: nothing a lie whose genuine outcome proves to be holy living. The criterion is one to which the present generation is partial; and whatever difficulties may attend its application, these words of Jesus are an ample recognition of its principle. Certainly, the Christian faith has no cause to fear the fair application of such a standard. Whether it stand ranged for judgment according to results alongside the Pagan and Mohammedan faiths of the world, or face to face with modern systems of infidelity, it can afford to abide the dispassionate verdict of history and of observation. Within Christendom itself, the reformed creed of Protestant nations need not decline, after three centuries of trial, to be tested by a comparison of its 'fruits' with those of Catholic theology. May we not narrow the area still more, and say: That type of evangelical Christianity which has done most for the production on a large scale of noble, heroic, and devout souls,

Of Detecting False Teachers in the Kingdom. 177

or which has prevailed to fashion pure, free, and healthy communities of men, capable of great things, is that which may claim to have received the gospel in its utmost integrity and to reflect with the greatest completeness the lessons of Jesus Christ? So far I think even irreligious critics may go in testing the substantial worth of evangelical faith by its historical effects on national prosperity and national character. But there are finer applications of this test, which every one is not competent to make. We need to be educated by Christianity itself, before we can quite recognise what are the noblest and most precious of those fruits we owe to Christ's regenerating grace— grapes of the kingdom which grow only on the true Vine, and are never to be found among the thorns which sin has planted in this smitten and unprofitable earth. That appreciation of holiness, in the christian sense, or power to discern what is spiritually 'good,' without which no one is fit to conduct such an inquiry, is itself a 'fruit' of the Spirit of Christ. Christianity, in fact, has created a standard for itself. To go beyond this, and attempt to discriminate between the tendencies of particular doctrines, or of such divergent views of divine truth as separate one section of the Evangelical Church from another,

PART II.

THIRD RELATION TO EVIL.

John xv. 1.

M

so as to test their theological accuracy by their supposed bearing on personal holiness, becomes a task too delicate for any save the wisest and best trained of spiritual Christians. Even in their hands, such an attempt may readily miscarry, through early bias or some personal preference. But differences in the apprehension of revealed truth which tell so faintly upon character, are by that very fact proved to be of subordinate moment. Any doctrine which can be called essential to the gospel of our salvation must be capable of reproducing itself powerfully in spiritual life. All such minor variations of opinion, therefore, as have emerged among evangelical believers, when viewed from this practical point of view, sink into insignificance beside that deep moral contrast which divides the fruits of vital Christianity, wherever found, from the fruits of unchristian and antichristian systems, when these are suffered to develope their influence on a sufficiently ample stage and through a sufficient period of dominance. It is by its fruits, after all, that the world has mainly 'known' or acknowledged the kingdom of Christ.

OF JUDGMENT ON EVIL WITHIN THE KINGDOM.

Not every one that saith unto Me, 'Lord, Lord,' shall enter into the Kingdom of Heaven; but he that doeth the will of My Father Which is in heaven. Many will say to Me in that day: 'Lord, Lord, have we not prophesied in Thy name? and in Thy name have cast out devils? and in Thy name done many wonderful works?' And then will I profess unto them: 'I never knew you; depart from Me, ye that work iniquity!'—MATT. VII. 21-23.   Cf. LUKE VI. 46, XIII. 25-27.

OF JUDGMENT ON EVIL WITHIN THE KINGDOM.

OUR Lord's sermon bends to its close. His words take here a wider range, and their tones gather a deeper solemnity. There is no essential change of subject at this point; it is still the same great law of which He speaks—a law as binding in morals as in physics: that the character of each kind of life is to be ascertained by its results. 'Judgment according to works' continues to be the keynote of His discourse. But while this one principle is common to the present and to the foregoing paragraph, there surely occurs a change, or an advance, in His application of the principle.[1] The image is dropped; and in dropping the image, there is a progress

PART II.

FOURTH RELATION TO EVIL.

Vers. 21-23 compared with vers. 15-20.

[1] The relation betwixt vers. 15-20 and vers. 21-23 has been variously apprehended by expositors; but Meyer is certainly less keen of observation than usual when he says (5th ed.): 'Nun giebt Jesus ohne Bild an, was Er mit seiner bildlichen Rede von den Fruchten gemeint hat.' How could the passage lead us on to the general lesson of vers. 24-27, if the reference was not widened from false prophets to all false professors whatever?

PART II.
FOURTH
RELATION TO
EVIL.

in the thought. The verses last considered apply to the present; these now before us to the future. Those refer to deceivers; these to the self-deceived. The former guide our judgment upon evil teachers who are found within God's kingdom in this world; but the latter describe the Lord's own judgment, and how He will finally shut evil men out of His kingdom hereafter. In the previous sentences, the reference was narrowed to a single class, such false teachers as we must test, since they will mislead us unless we beware of them; but now His language widens to embrace all professed subjects of His kingdom whose lives are inconsistent with their profession. Hitherto, Jesus has been speaking as the Founder of His Church; now He speaks as its final Judge.

So unexpected an enlargement of the application which is made of the great principle just reasserted,[1] necessitates a remarkable change in the tone and attitude of the Preacher. Hitherto, He has sat quietly among the crowd, clad only with a gentle dignity, and speaking words of human lowliness. Blessings have dropped from

---

[1] The principle is repeated in ver. 20, which, while it looks back to and rehearses ver. 16a, forms really a new starting-point for ver. 21 ff.

His lips. Even in legislating for His new kingdom, He has been content to interpret the ancient statute-law of Israel, to develope its spirit, and to trace afresh its bearing on the every-day life of society. He has stooped to gather lessons of cheer for the toiling poor from flower and bird. He has encouraged us to speak to God like children who ask bread from their father. All His words have been most human, full of earthly pictures, and considerately adapted to our infirmities; even when at the end they have grown sharp with a call to self-denial, or solemn with a warning against lying leaders. But now, of a sudden, He carries His congregation forward with Him at a leap to the far-off end of all things and the awful day of universal trial. He reaches forth into the unknown destinies of men; lifts the veil, forbidden to mortal hands, which conceals our final doom; seats Himself upon the dread tribunal of the Omniscient; and, in brief dialogue which shakes the hearer's heart with terror, rehearses the transactions and foretells the irrevocable sentence of the judgment-day. As though the hill-side grass had been transformed into 'a great white throne,' and His Galilean peasant garb into robes of flame! What wonder if the hushed multitude crouched in silence that

PART II.

FOURTH RELATION TO EVIL.

See Rev. xx. 11, i. 13-15.

might be felt, while His slow words of doom fell one by one upon their ears! What wonder if, when all was ended, they whispered fearfully to each other: 'He speaks like One Who hath authority!'

On a later occasion, at greater length, and with ampler pomp and circumstance of description, our Lord foretold the final segregation of good and evil members within His visible kingdom, in language which left no shadow of doubt that He claimed for Himself the awful function of the Judge of quick and dead. The apostolic doctrine, that it is 'before the judgment-seat of Christ' we must all appear, has therefore the most abundant and unequivocal foundation in the teaching of Jesus Himself. But this prodigious claim is as really advanced in these briefer words of the Sermon on the Mount as in that later passage. Here, just as there, He puts Himself in the front as the Judge. Here, just as there, it is to Him the self-deceived allege their grounds of hope; here, as there, it is His voice which bids the unrighteous 'depart.' Yet here it occurs to close and crown a discourse, which, of all His long discourses recorded, is the most human and (so to say) natural in its tone; which, in fact, has hardly until now betrayed by

Of Judgment on Evil within the Kingdom. 185

any syllable that the Speaker claimed to be more than a mortal prophet, a second and, at most, a greater Moses. It is impossible to deal fairly with even these words of Jesus, without owning that He assumed to be, in a sense which separated Him from all other men, supernatural and divine.

This amazing pretension to sit in the seat of God and adjudicate on the ultimate fate of human beings, is made more, not less, impressive, by its being so quietly taken for granted, rather than obtruded upon our attention. The truth is, it is only introduced at all with a purely practical or hortatory design. It is not of Himself the Preacher is thinking when He pictures Himself as detecting His false subjects, but of them. Their perilous mistake; their self-delusion; their exposure when too late; their final expulsion from the kingdom: these are the terrible facts which fill His vision and kindle His imagination. To warn every so-called Christian how he must in the end have his profession tested by his conduct, and by the terrors of that ordeal to shake deceived souls out of their dream of security, and shut them up into that narrow path of holiness which alone conducts to life: this is the merciful design which inspires His forecast of judgment. Perhaps this

PART II.

FOURTH
RELATION TO
EVIL.

design may explain to us the dramatic form into which, here as elsewhere, our Lord has cast His anticipations of the ultimate tribunal. He may have chosen the dialogue dress in order to make the delusive anticipations of these professors and their fearful undeceiving stand forth with a vividness and lifelike effect, which could have been attained by no abstract statement; while, at the same time, such a dramatic dressing of the facts could deceive no one, as though it gave any literal account of a mighty moral transaction, the precise details of which must be for the present concealed from human view. Both here and in the later passage there is as little as possible said to satisfy mere curiosity, or to betray prematurely the actual form or method of final judgment. But the moral warning intended by the Preacher, and for the sake of which He was pleased to raise in any degree the curtain of the future, is thrown up (so to speak) upon the surface in such relief that the most heedless or unwilling eye cannot fail to see it.

To this fresh and wider warning, left by the King to be laid to heart by all those professed subjects of His kingdom whom He is one day to judge, our attention must now be called.

It is right that we should scrutinize the pretensions of teachers who come to us in Christ's name, professing to guide us in Christ's path. To judge such men by their fruits is right, simply because it is necessary for our own safety. That we may not be misled by 'false prophets,' we must, for our personal satisfaction at least, 'try the spirits whether they are of God.' This special case, however, does not invalidate the wider law, that we 'judge not.' While we are to be on our guard against unchristian doctrine, the detection or exposure of pretended Christians is not in our hands. There is an obvious difference between the man who affects to lead me in the way of life, and whose claims I must therefore judge before I can follow him, and the man who simply styles himself a private disciple of Christ. With the true or false profession of such fellow-Christians as only claim to keep me company in the narrow way, it is no business of mine to meddle. Rather, the thing for me to remember in this connection is, that they and I are alike on our way to the face of One Who will in the end try all of us. When I renounce the forbidden office of judge of my neighbour's Christianity, it is because I remember that he is no judge of mine, but that both of us have One That judgeth us.

PART II.

FOURTH RELATION TO EVIL.

1 John iv. 1.

Matt. vii. 1.

Now, in thus enlarging the area of judgment from 'false prophets' to professing Christians, and in removing the task of judgment out of our hands to Christ's, and in postponing the time of judgment till the Great Day; there is, be it observed, no change or relaxation in the rule of judgment. All that our Lord has taught us, under the former paragraph, about the difference betwixt a profession which can be put on, and 'fruits' which really grow out of the heart; and how the former may readily deceive the eye if not checked by the sure test of the latter; all this we can transfer to the wider and remoter judgment of the Christ upon His whole kingdom. The criterion He has prescribed to us where we meanwhile need to judge, is the criterion by which in the end He will judge us all; and the unreliable assumed cloak of righteousness in which He bids us have no confidence when we find another wearing it, is a cloak which will stand us in poor stead when we ourselves appear before His own inspection. Not sheep-skin covering, but the honest fruits of character, will carry us into His kingdom; not saying, 'Lord, Lord,' but doing His Father's will.

There is no less need, then, to guard ourselves against self-deception than against deceivers.

Nay, self-deception is the more perilous of the two; since it is less likely to be detected by ourselves or to be exposed by any other, before that fatal day, when its exposure is certain indeed to come, but will come too late. Here and there, from age to age, a few lying prophets may creep into Christ's fold whom it will need some care to know for wolves; but that is a rare and a patent danger, compared to the 'many' who attach themselves to the crowd of His nominal subjects, and are as forward as any others to avow loyalty to His name, yet under this garb of discipleship conceal even from themselves a disobedient and worldly heart. Such an exterior show of attachment to Christ may even be both very ingenuous and very easily mistaken for reality. To say 'Lord, Lord,' is no more than every disciple must do: it is the simple acknowledgment in words of Jesus' Messiahship —the earliest badge of membership in His Church — the primitive confession of faith. 'Every one' says that; but of those who say it, there are 'many' who go a great deal further. Three stages are distinguished in our Lord's words; or perhaps three classes of the self-deluded: Prophets, who exercise their gifts in the public congregation to the edification of their

PART II.

FOURTH RELATION TO EVIL.

πολλοί, ver. 22.

Christian brethren; Exorcists, who, by invoking the saving might of Christ, have delivered possessed men from evil influences; Wonder-workers, who seem to themselves and others to wield a quite supernatural power through their exceptional piety. And in every case, the disciple is forward to avow that his spiritual performances rest upon the presence and assistance of the Lord Jesus Christ: he does everything in that prevailing name. These examples are certainly not overstated. Such exhibitions of pseudo-spiritual power have often been familiar to the Church. In the apostolic age, when believers in their assemblies edified one another by mutual exhortation, the gift of excited and moving speech was no sure mark of grace. Not all who 'took upon them to call over them which had evil spirits the name of the Lord Jesus' were such deliberate impostors or so readily confuted as the seven sons of Sceva. St. Paul seems to have found it a possible thing for a man to 'have all faith, so that he could remove mountains,' and yet not have charity. Nor is it only in the primitive Church that such phenomena have appeared. Other periods, characterized by a like intense spiritual fervour joined to scant discrimination, have supplied similar instances to

Marginalia:
PART II.
FOURTH RELATION TO EVIL.

'In Thy name,' three times in ver. 22. Cf. Acts iii. 6, 16, iv. 10, 17, 30, xvi. 18, etc.

See Acts xix. 13-17.

1 Cor. xiii. 1-3.

the candid student of spiritual disease; instances which enable us to understand our Lord in the most literal sense. Wherever religious excitement runs high, it is apt to carry on its tide impressible natures, profoundly moved in their emotional sentiments and in their imagination, without being touched to the quick of conscience, or really begotten again to a divine passion for righteousness. Such unhappy persons are often borne along under an excitement which is really due to mixed influences, but which they mistake for the genuine breath of God. A false conceit of being eminent organs of the Divine Spirit inflates them with the worst kind of pride. Then the excitement, which at its outset was real enough, however superficial, becomes unhealthy and insincere. Under the stimulus of vanity, they lose moral self-control. In a superstitious age they develope into devotees, saintly ascetics, fanatics, and miracle-mongers. Meanwhile conscience is drugged and silent. Sometimes, indeed, such a morbid religious development may be found to rest upon a base of genuine piety. More often, the narrow way of self-denial and lowly obedience and patient wisdom—the only safe way for human feet—has never been entered through the strait gate of penitence; yet the wretched soul, wondered at by the ignorant and flattered for a saint, dreams of heaven all down the broad road, till the terrible awaking comes at last!

No doubt these are extreme cases; though something analogous may be seen, thrown off like foam by every great religious movement. But by such extreme cases, does not our Lord design to warn us against trusting to any experience, supposed to be spiritual, or taken for conversion, which does not involve as its very pith and kernel a profound moral change from sin to virtue, or which fails to justify itself in the long run by a life of enduring practical goodness? 'The kingdom of God is not meat and drink;' not Pharisaic scrupulosity in external observances. As little is it emotional fervour, whether vented in groans or praises; or 'striking' experiences; or zeal for the Gospel; or a power to talk with unction, and edify and warm the listener. No; it is simply and entirely 'righteousness:' that is its fruit, its proper product, its only infallible test. To 'do the will of the Father,' as His Son has in this Sermon been expounding it to us; to do it out of a pure heart, as in His sight, and with perfect love as our inspiring motive: that is what proves any of

Of Judgment on Evil within the Kingdom.

us to be a disciple of Christ, and nothing else but that can prove it. Forward to our King's tribunal the current of our life is carrying each of us; before that tribunal we shall find that we have left behind us everything else in which we trusted, and must vindicate our relationship to the King Himself by the practical issues of our life in conduct, and by that alone. Surely it is a very solemn light which is thus shed back from the seat of final trial over all those laws and duties of Christ's New Testament kingdom which fill the major portion of this regal manifesto. The Gospel is not all a thing of promise or of benediction. Its message opens with a sevenfold blessing; but it ends with judgment. The Gospel holds a law wrapt up within its bosom. The prescripts of this King are harder to be kept than those of Moses. These severe commands: to fulfil every jot of duty, to be as perfect as God, to act in His sight and not men's, to seek His kingdom before gold, to do to all as we desire them to do to us: these commands, I say, are meant to be obeyed; and they are not matters to be done at a rush, under some passing heat of sentiment, or in a glow of Sunday enthusiasm, when warmed with eloquence; but they are plain, hard, imperious, constant duties;

PART II.

FOURTH RELATION TO EVIL.

Cf. John xii. 47, 48.

v. 18, 48; vi. 1, 33; vii. 12.

N

a most strict way of life, in which we must be found walking by sun and shade, on Sunday and week-day, both when our feet trip lightly along the path and when we need to urge reluctant steps up an unwelcome steep with our teeth set and only dogged necessity holding us to our task. These are duties, too, with no *éclat* attending them; they minister in no wise to spiritual elation; they are too frigid and commonplace for overstrained pietism or ultra-devout people of any sort. They fall to be done by quiet everyday and unobtrusive acts of justice and kindness and hidden self-control—by trifling sacrifices and very homely toil—by the silent relinquishment, now of pleasure and anon of gain, for the approval of Him Who seeth in secret. Nor are we incited to these duties only by promises of reward such as were held out at an earlier stage. It is not at our option whether we shall toil to earn by obedience the Father's approval. These things we must do, or be reprobate. We must do them, on peril of forfeiting salvation. We must do them, or hear in the end from the lips of unspeakable grace words so terrible as these: 'Depart from Me, ye that work iniquity.'

By a single word, our Lord has given us a key,

as I think, to this evangelical value of good works as a test of christian profession. What self-deceived members of His Church advance in evidence of their claim to eternal life consists entirely in certain outward relations which they have sustained to Jesus Christ. They have called Him 'Lord;' they have prophesied in His name; they have exorcised and wrought marvels. These things they allege as signs of very close and intimate relations betwixt Him and them. Now, if such things really implied any vital or inward bond between the man and Christ, as the deceived professors imagine, their claim to eternal life would be made out. But it is precisely here that their delusion lies. The Judge will undeceive them. He will frankly 'confess' to them—what it has been the blame and the misery of such people not to have cared to learn before—how the case really stands. The truth is, there has never been betwixt them and Him any friendly intimacy or communion whatever. 'Then will I confess unto them: "I never knew you."' This pregnant use of the knowledge which one person has of another, to intimate a friendly intercourse between them on the basis of community in interest and sympathy, has its roots in ancient Hebrew usage. It is not without

PART II.
FOURTH RELATION TO EVIL.

ὁμολογήσω. ver. 23, translated 'profess.'

Cf. Nahum i. 7; see John x. 14.

PART II.
FOURTH
RELATION TO
EVIL.
e.g. Gal. iv. 9;
cf. 1 Cor. viii.
3, c. xiii. 12;
and see especially 2 Tim.
ii. 19.

parallel even in Jesus' language. It is rather frequent with St. Paul. It reposes on the principle that no living person can be truly and fully understood without love. As St. Paul puts it, it is the man who loves God who (not only can be said to know God, but even) is really known of Him. When the Judge, therefore, to put the deceived right, shall 'confess' that, in the true sense of the word, He has had no personal knowledge of them in spite of their free use of His name, He gives us a key to the difference between such pseudo-spiritual actions as they allege and such ethical 'fruit' as He demands. Whatever may be done by a man without personal union to Jesus Christ in faith and love, or without such communion with Him as implies a full friendly accord in sympathy and motive: that is only the imitation of christian life—a sheepskin Christianity borrowed and worn upon the outside of character, without implying real christian life within. On the other hand, it is impossible to have come into personal relations of friendliness with Christ, to have learned to sympathize with His mission and to live by faith upon Him as one's Saviour and Lord, without receiving a new moral life which must discover itself in character. The holy passion of Jesus

Christ for righteousness, His imitation of the Father, His zeal for human recovery, His self-sacrificing charity, His loyalty to law: these are ground-features of His character as the Son of God, which cannot fail to be reproduced in every soul who inheres or 'abides' in His communion after any genuine or spiritual fashion. To be in inner fellowship with Him is to be, in His own words, a branch growing upon the gracious and fruitful Vine, and every such branch must bear the grapes of God. *[margin: Cf. John xv. 1-8.]*

When the words of Jesus are searched, then, and His thought pushed back to its basis, it will be found that the difference between those who only believe themselves to be Christians and those who are Christians, is this, that the one class have, and the other have not, a spiritual life, rooted in personal union with Christ, and discovering itself in conduct resembling His own. On another occasion, later in His ministry, our Lord appears to have repeated substantially the words here employed; but on that occasion He added an expression, preserved by St. Luke, which hints to us how profoundly contrasted in the origin of their moral life are the true and the false professors of His name. 'I tell you,' is the language to be addressed to those who shall *[margin: Luke xiii. 25-27. So Olshausen, in loc.]*

[margin top: PART II. FOURTH RELATION TO EVIL.]

PART II.

FOURTH RELATION TO EVIL.

knock in vain at the door of His celestial home: 'I tell you, I know you not *whence ye are.*' The life whose connection with Christ is only external, owns in reality a foreign origin; its source is elsewhere; its moral parentage is the opposite from divine: Christ therefore knows not whence it is. But he who is one with Christ by a spiritual birth has a life derived from God; and of that life the issues are righteous deeds. 'If ye know (is the comment of St. John) that He is righteous, ye know that every one that doeth righteousness is born of Him.' 'In this,' therefore, 'the children of God are manifested, and the children of the devil: whosoever doeth not righteousness is not of God.'

Cf. John viii. 34-44.

1 John ii. 29, iii. 10.

Cf. Matt. xii. 33.

So that, after all, the tree must be first made good, before its fruit can be good: only it is by the goodness of its fruit that the goodness of the tree is known. In the Master's teaching lies the solution of that old evangelical antinomy betwixt faith and works. But His scholars James and Paul do not differ; they agree. Faith precedes works, and produces works, and by works is 'made perfect;' so St. James teaches. Faith works by love, and love fulfils the law: this is the teaching of St. Paul. Faith that works no fruit is dead; works that are not wrought by

Jas. ii. 22.

Gal. v. 6; Rom. xiii. 10.

faith are dead also. Life lies in the union of soul and body: of inward devotion and outward character. It is an idle quarrel which has been waged betwixt the partisans of either side of the shield. When St. Paul was old, he taught his son Timothy that the seal of God which attests the foundation of our christian hope has two sides; and if its obverse bears for a motto these words of the Judge: 'The Lord knoweth them that are His;' there is also on its reverse this legend which he who runs may read: 'Let every one that nameth the name of Christ depart from iniquity.'

CONCLUSION.

Therefore, whosoever heareth these sayings of Mine, and doeth them, I will liken him unto a wise man, which built his house upon a rock; and the rain descended, and the floods came, and the winds blew, and beat upon that house; and it fell not: for it was founded upon a rock. And every one that heareth these sayings of Mine, and doeth them not, shall be likened unto a foolish man, which built his house upon the sand; and the rain descended, and the floods came, and the winds blew, and beat upon that house; and it fell: and great was the fall of it.—MATT. VII. 24–27.

Cf. LUKE VI. 46–49. *And why call ye Me, 'Lord, Lord,' and do not the things which I say? Whosoever cometh to Me, and heareth My sayings, and doeth them, I will show you to whom he is like: he is like a man which built an house, and digged deep, and laid the foundation on a rock: and when the flood arose, the stream beat vehemently upon that house, and could not shake it; for it was founded upon a rock* [or, *well-built*]. *But he that heareth, and doeth not, is like a man that, without a foundation, built an house upon the earth; against which the stream did beat vehemently, and immediately it fell; and the ruin of that house was great.*

CONCLUSION.

AS every good peroration should, this peroration of our Lord's great Sermon both springs immediately out of the foregoing train of thought, and also looks back over the whole discourse to sum up its leading lesson.

The startling fact, which He Who is to be Judge as well as Lawgiver has just been pealing in His disciples' ears, is this: that men can go far and long in a simulated discipleship, without knowing it, till before His seat of judgment they find it out too late. This is what has made the closing paragraph of the Sermon rattle like a crash of near thunder. And because such judgment on disciples is to go at last by the evidence of deeds, 'therefore' the man who hears only, without doing, the words of Jesus, is a 'fool.' To expose the folly of such disobedient hearers is plainly the purpose of the peroration. At the same time, the backward glance over 'these sayings of Mine,' seems to gather up the long series of instructions over which we have been

PART II.
CONCLUSION.

travelling, into the unity of a code. This mountain Sermon is one. Its 'sayings' have a common principle. They constitute one legislative act for the guidance of citizens in the new kingdom of God. They are a law to be kept in its integrity, if kept aright at all. They will be kept by every true citizen who has the spirit of the kingdom and the love of the King within him. By others they will not be kept. They will only be listened to. But how intensely practical a thing is Christianity in the eyes of Christ! The whole drift and movement of this long discourse has carried us forward with it to one most weighty practical conclusion,—which here, like a stone swung at the sling's end, is discharged full upon us with crushing momentum,—that, after all, *he only is a Christian who does what Christ bids him.*

This closing lesson of the entire discourse is rendered impressive and memorable, not only by the vivid double simile under which it is conveyed, but still more even by the full round roll of the style; the intentional repetition of the same phrases in both halves of the parable; the continuous solemn sweep of the long redoubled sentence which seems to dwell upon the ear, and afterwards to haunt the memory. The materials of the picture were familiar to His audience. Syrian houses of the poorer class were then probably (as they still are) very slight—built of mud or a few unhewn stones, roughly daubed with 'untempered mortar,' and roofed in by no stouter materials than brushwood with a layer of grass-grown earth over it. Two such houses have been erected in one of the precipitous wadys which everywhere seam the limestone ranges of Palestine, and swiftly drain off its superfluous rainfall. So long as summer lasts and the bed of the watercourse is dry, both of them stand equally well and appear to be equally secure. But a day of testing comes. One of those terrific storms of rain and hail which the treacherous winds of the Levant bring up suddenly from the sea, swells the brook in a few hours into a torrent; and when the flood sweeps down its narrow channel like a tide, turbid and white with foam from one rocky bank to the other, while the fierce rain-storm drives up the ravine before the western gale, and lashes on roof and sides, then is put to proof the stability of both dwellings; then everything depends on the character of their foundation. The one has been built, with careless want of foresight, upon nothing better than the layer of loose sand or gravel

PART II. CONCLUSION.
Cf. Ezek. xiii. 10–16.
See Ps. cxxix. 6; Mark ii. 4.
Cf. πλημμύρα in Luke.

brought down by former floods. Of course, the waters which eddy now about its base fret away from beneath it the very soil on which it stands, till the force of the storm, beating down upon its undermined and unsupported walls, crushes it into ruin. It was a 'refuge of lies,' for it pretended to a foundation which it had not; and 'the overflowing scourge' rolls it indignantly to the sea. The other builder, on the contrary, when he began to build, took the precaution to clear away that drift sand, deep though it was, and, digging down to the rock beneath, laid his foundation there. Now he finds the reward of his prudent pains and thoroughness. The flood may wash away, no doubt, whatever is moveable from about the base of his house, even as from his neighbour's; but when its walls are laid bare to the very rock, the secret strength of his 'hiding-place' is only discovered to view: and though roof and sides may suffer here and there in their weaker portions from the searching of wind or rain, yet his house at least, as a place to shelter him, is secure from demolition: it falls not, for it is founded on the rock.

So Jesus leaves His parable to interpret itself. The contrast betwixt a superficial profession of discipleship, in which self-deceived Christians confide as sufficient, and that thoroughgoing, profound moral earnestness which is concerned to make sure work of it, and to be all that it seems to be: this lies on the surface of the parable, and perhaps this is all that in the first instance was apparent to the hearers of it. It is foolish to forget that a day of trial is at hand, when conduct only will stand the test of God; foolish to hear Christ's word, and call Christ 'Lord,' and fancy that a reputation for discipleship, based on such a flimsy foundation as this, will always shelter you from the storm. The disciple who would be really safe, must go deeper to work with his religion than that. He must rest his christian profession on the solid ground of heart earnestness after righteousness; he must thoroughly be what he appears; he must do what he hears. So far, I say, the meaning lies on the surface. But when we recall what use had been made of this same metaphor before, what use was to be made of it later, it seems not unreasonable to find in our Lord's words something more than this. That moral thoroughness in the christian life which aims at consistent obedience to Christ, succeeds in doing His word only by coming into close and trustful contact with Himself. He who would be practically a Christian, must have nothing betwixt his naked soul and the eternal Rock, Christ; for it is only as based on Him, fastened to Him, that any disciple learns to love His word, or gets strength to do it. In the very passage of prophecy to which Jesus seems to be here alluding, it is the man whose confidence is built upon the tried and precious Stone, laid of God in Zion, whose refuge is not swept away by the hail when God makes righteousness His plummet of judgment. In that apostolic passage, too, where St. Paul seems most closely to imitate these sentences of his Master,—though the trial of the final day is figured not as a test by water, but as a test by fire, and though all we build is not supposed to stand that test,—it is still Jesus Christ Who is the one foundation laid. The truth is, that these two thoughts are in scriptural teaching, as in actual fact, inseparable : no christian life will stand the last judgment of God which is not in practical conformity with the laws of Christ; and no christian life can be in conformity with Christ's laws which is not rooted in personal spiritual union with Christ Himself. Sometimes it is the one, sometimes the other, of these two which is uppermost with the sacred writers; but always where the other is

Margin notes: PART II. CONCLUSION. Isa. xxviii. *ut supra*, c. 1 Pet. ii. 4–8. 1 Cor. iii. *ut supra*.

uppermost, the other lies underneath. In the parable before us they seem to coalesce.

PART II.
CONCLUSION.

Days are often coming in the lives of all of us which try the worth of our Christianity. Days of unlooked-for losses or days of sudden elevation or enrichment, may either of them become for a man a time of exposure, when the bad foundation gives way before the temptation to abandon Christ, and one's life-long profession of religion crumbles visibly before men's eyes. Better so, than await in the fancied security of the fool the oncoming of that final 'day' of which all other judgment days are only feeble types and partial foretellings! Swiftly, on the wings of every dawn, comes that last of dawns. A day of more searching tempest, of more destructive fire; it shall leave no false claim unconsumed, no baseless hope unruined. 'A prudent man foreseeth the evil, and hideth himself: but the simple pass on and are punished.' Let us look each one to his foundation. There are so many who seem to be taking their stand for eternity on Jesus Christ: there are possibly so few whose lives are built into the Rock. So many of us hear, so few are manifestly doing, His words. Now surely is a time, if ever there was one, for trumpeting in the ears of the

Prov. xxii. 3 (repeated in xxvii. 12).

o

PART II.
CONCLUSION.
Jas. i. 22.

Church what St. James trumpeted to his own age, in words which sound like a reverberation of his Master's: 'BE YE DOERS OF THE WORD, AND NOT HEARERS ONLY, DECEIVING YOUR OWN SELVES.'

THE END.

MURRAY AND GIBB, EDINBURGH,
PRINTERS TO HER MAJESTY'S STATIONERY OFFICE.

www.ingramcontent.com/pod-product-compliance
Lightning Source LLC
Chambersburg PA
CBHW020826230426
43666CB00007B/1123